THE CASTAWAYS

BLUESMAN
BOOK THREE
ROB VOLLMAR & PABLO G. CALLEJO

BROWNSVILLE
kleid & jake allen
CANDY
DELI

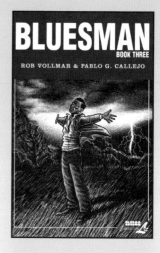

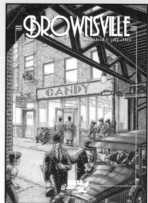

THE CASTAWAYS

Rob Vollmar
Pablo G. Callejo

ISBN 10: 1-56163-492-1, hardcover
ISBN 13: 978-1-56163-492-7, hardcover
ISBN 10: 1-56163-493-X, paperback
ISBN 13: 978-1-56163-493-4, paperback

ComicsLit is an imprint
and trademark of

NANTIER • BEALL • MINOUSTCHINE
Publishing inc.
new york

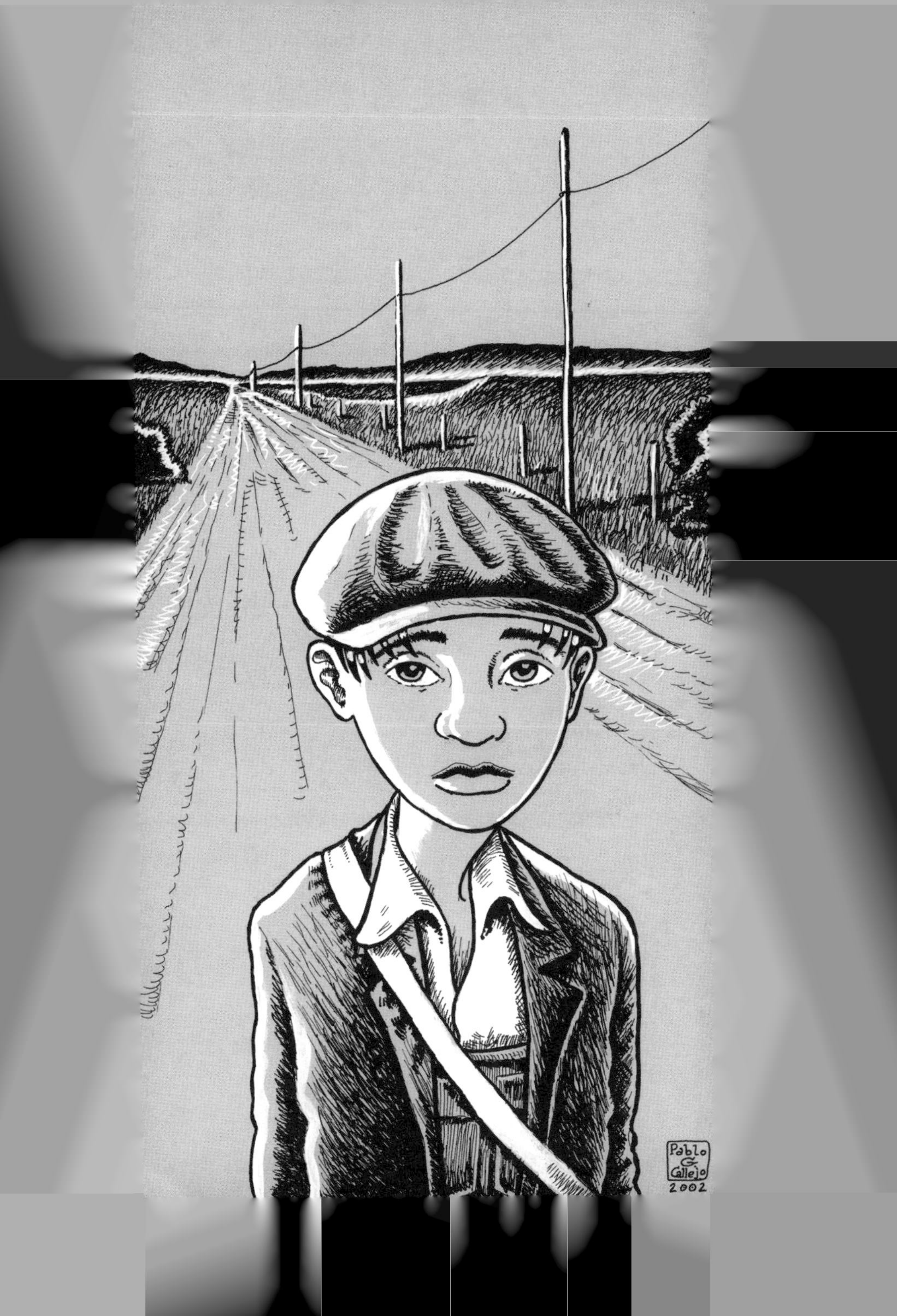
Pablo G. Callejo
2002

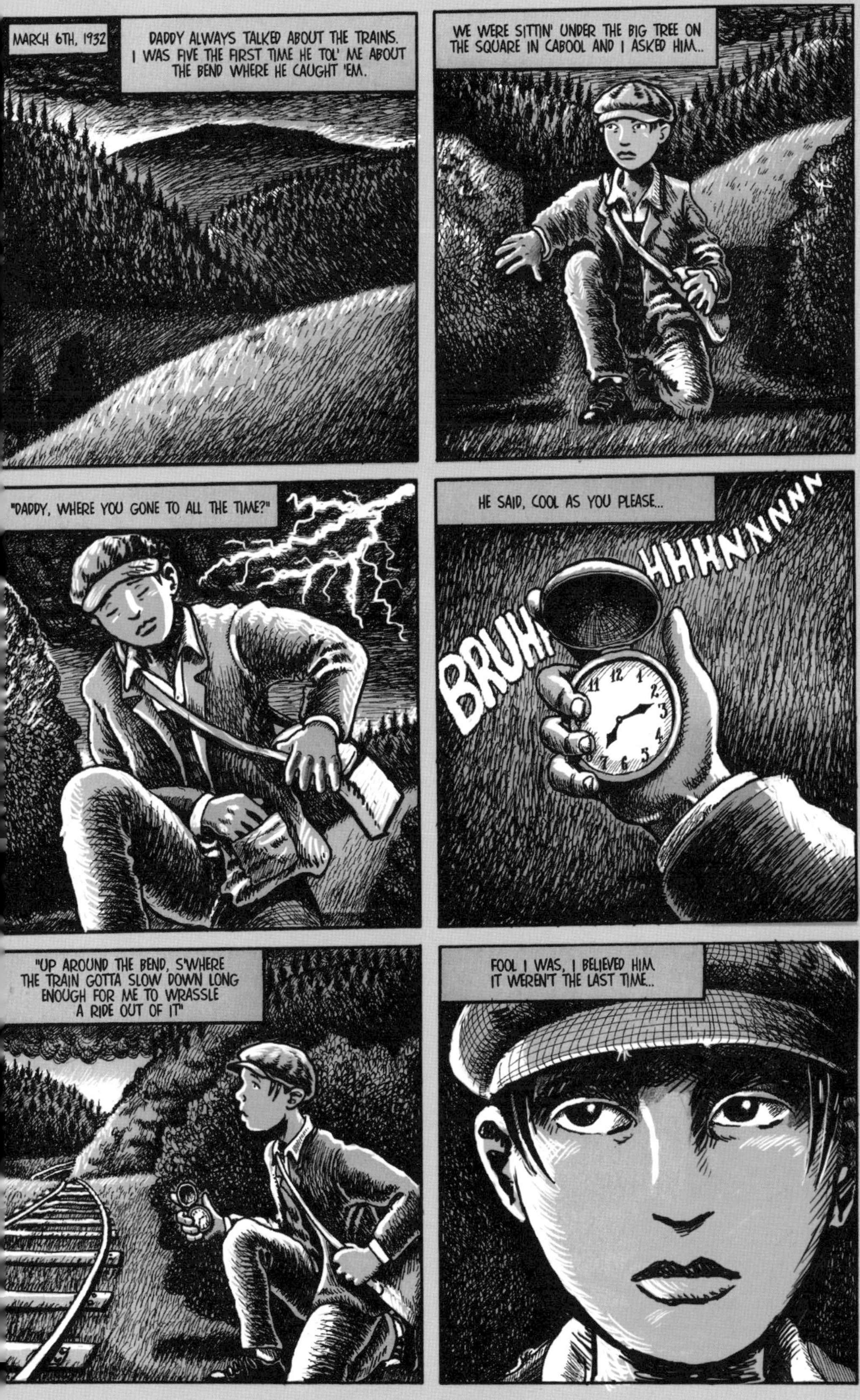
MARCH 6TH, 1932
DADDY ALWAYS TALKED ABOUT THE TRAINS. I WAS FIVE THE FIRST TIME HE TOL' ME ABOUT THE BEND WHERE HE CAUGHT 'EM.
WE WERE SITTIN' UNDER THE BIG TREE ON THE SQUARE IN CABOOL AND I ASKED HIM..
"DADDY, WHERE YOU GONE TO ALL THE TIME?"
HE SAID, COOL AS YOU PLEASE...
BRUHHHHNNNNNN
"UP AROUND THE BEND, S'WHERE THE TRAIN GOTTA SLOW DOWN LONG ENOUGH FOR ME TO WRASSLE A RIDE OUT OF IT"
FOOL I WAS, I BELIEVED HIM IT WEREN'T THE LAST TIME...

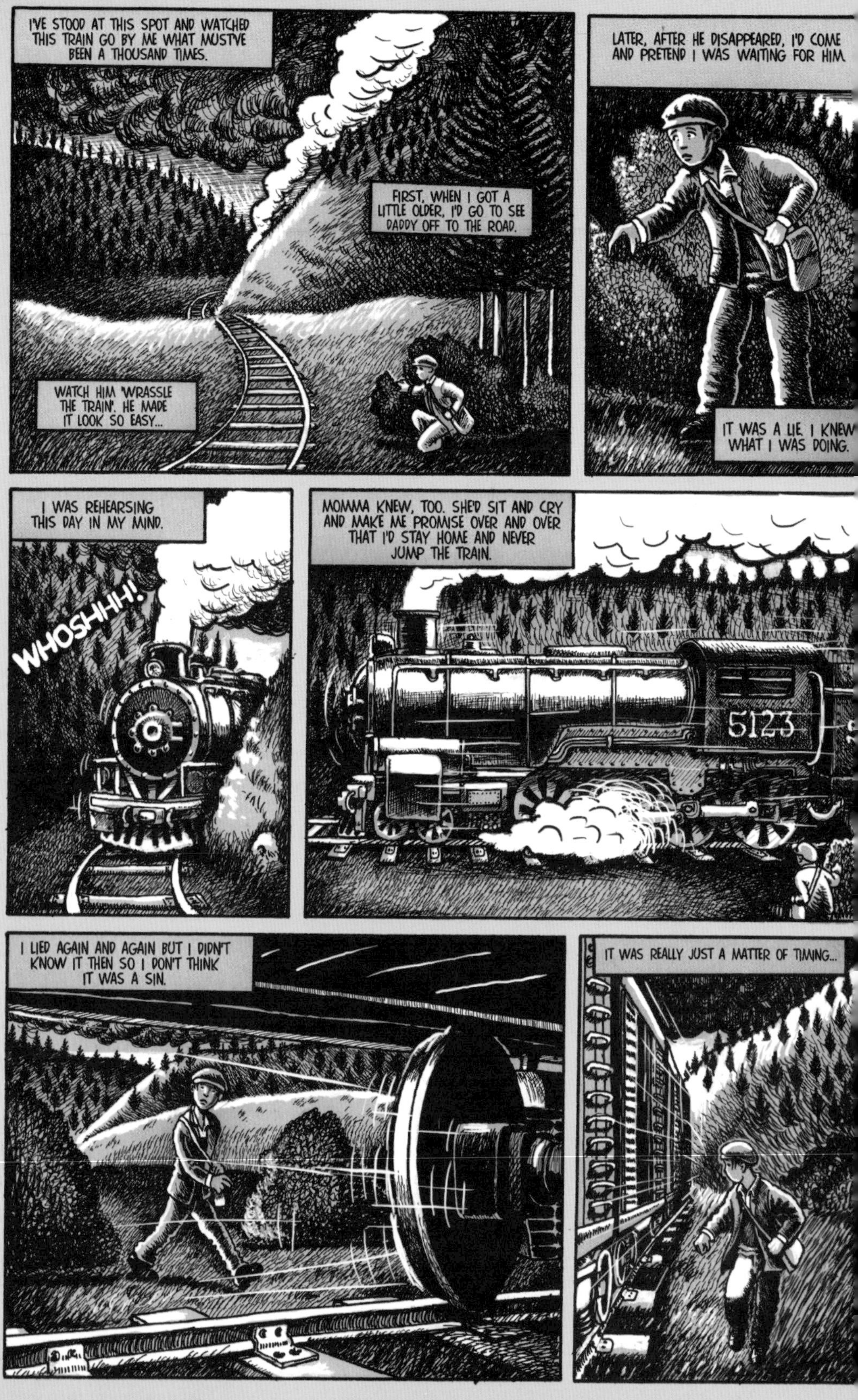
I'VE STOOD AT THIS SPOT AND WATCHED THIS TRAIN GO BY ME WHAT MUST'VE BEEN A THOUSAND TIMES.
FIRST, WHEN I GOT A LITTLE OLDER, I'D GO TO SEE DADDY OFF TO THE ROAD.
WATCH HIM 'WRASSLE THE TRAIN'. HE MADE IT LOOK SO EASY...
LATER, AFTER HE DISAPPEARED, I'D COME AND PRETEND I WAS WAITING FOR HIM.
IT WAS A LIE. I KNEW WHAT I WAS DOING.
I WAS REHEARSING THIS DAY IN MY MIND.
WHOSHHH!
MOMMA KNEW, TOO. SHE'D SIT AND CRY AND MAKE ME PROMISE OVER AND OVER THAT I'D STAY HOME AND NEVER JUMP THE TRAIN.
5123
I LIED AGAIN AND AGAIN BUT I DIDN'T KNOW IT THEN SO I DON'T THINK IT WAS A SIN.
IT WAS REALLY JUST A MATTER OF TIMING...

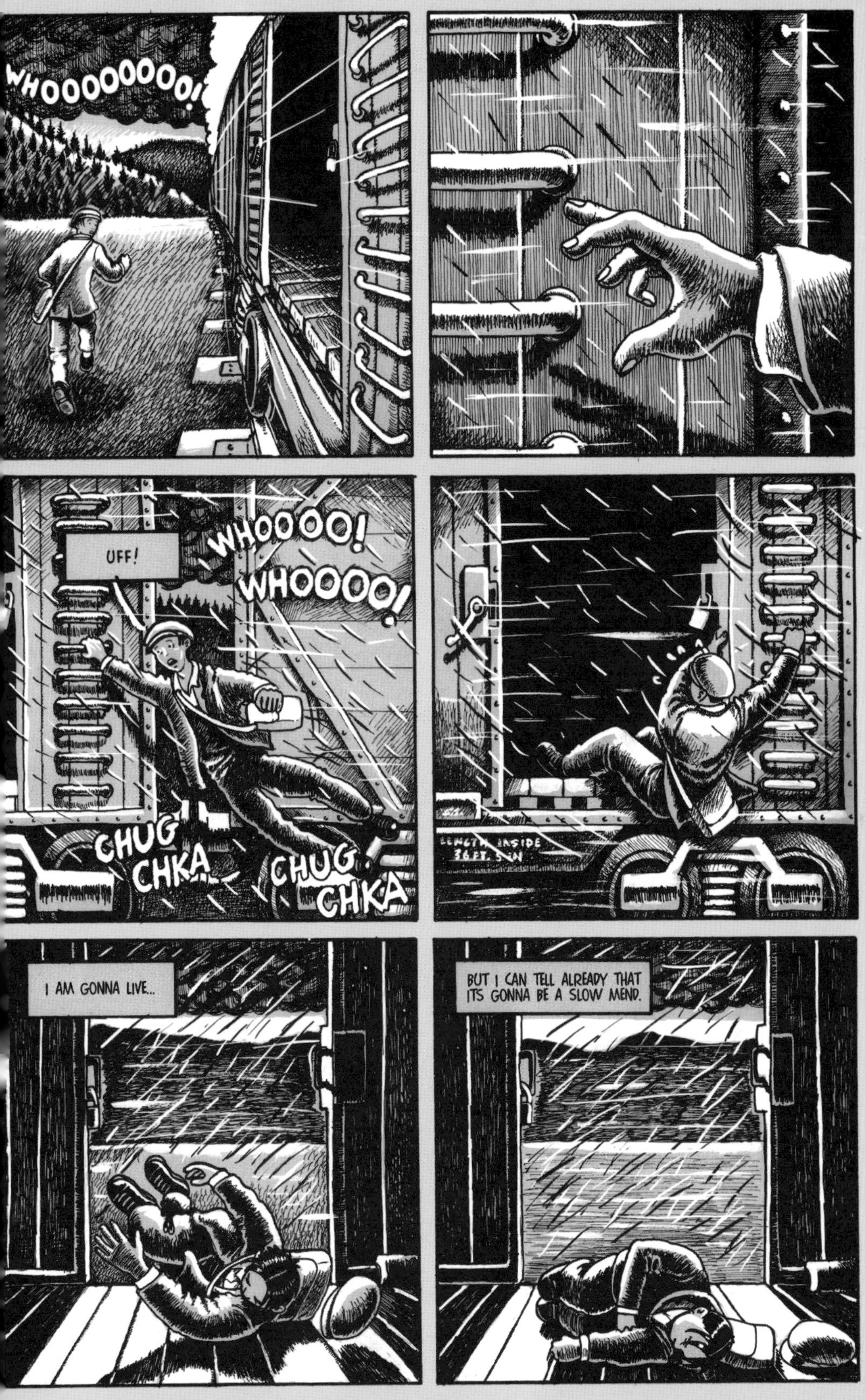
WHOOOOOOOO!
UFF!
WHOOOO!
WHOOOO!
CHUG
CHKA
CHUG
CHKA
I AM GONNA LIVE...
BUT I CAN TELL ALREADY THAT ITS GONNA BE A SLOW MEND.

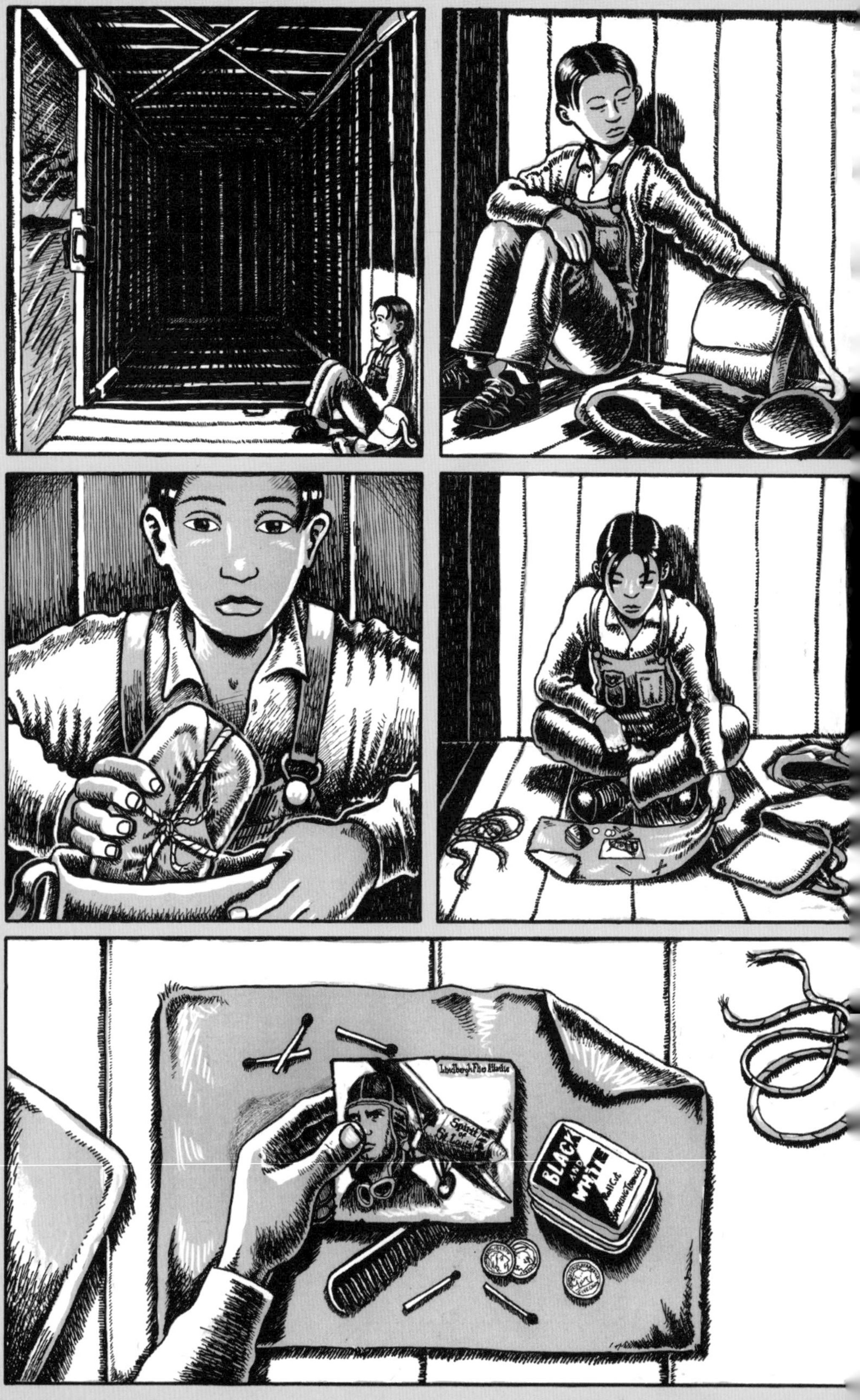
Spirit of St. Louis
BLACK AND WHITE
Roll Cut
SMOKING TOBACCO

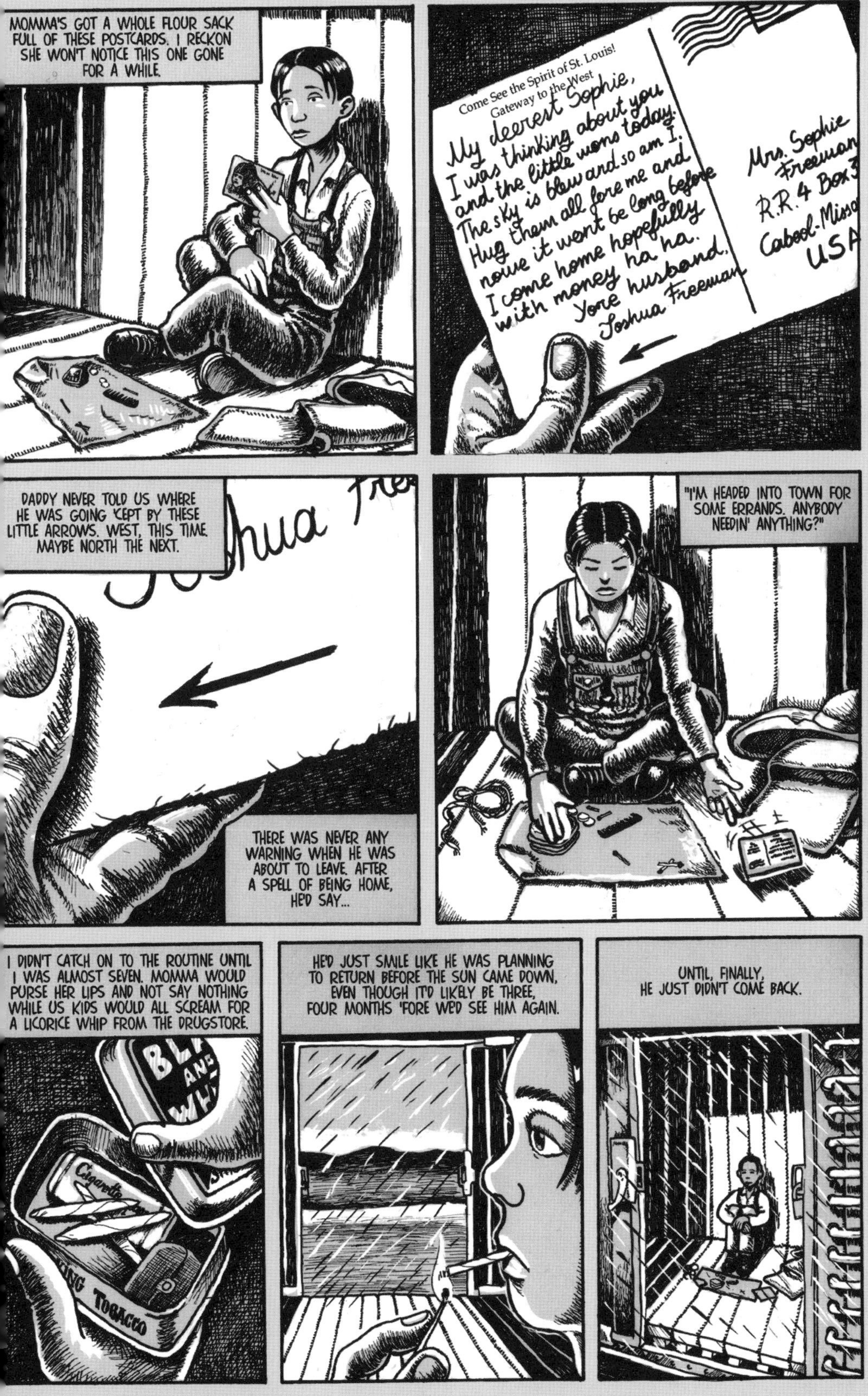
MOMMA'S GOT A WHOLE FLOUR SACK FULL OF THESE POSTCARDS. I RECKON SHE WON'T NOTICE THIS ONE GONE FOR A WHILE.
Come See the Spirit of St. Louis!
Gateway to the West
My deerest Sophie,
I was thinking about you
and the little wons today.
The sky is blew and so am I.
Hug them all fore me and
nowe it wont be long before
I come home hopefully
with money ha ha.
Yore husband,
Joshua Freeman
Mrs. Sophie
Freeman
R.R. 4 Box 3
Cabool-Miss
USA
DADDY NEVER TOLD US WHERE HE WAS GOING 'CEPT BY THESE LITTLE ARROWS. WEST, THIS TIME. MAYBE NORTH THE NEXT.
THERE WAS NEVER ANY WARNING WHEN HE WAS ABOUT TO LEAVE. AFTER A SPELL OF BEING HOME, HE'D SAY...
"I'M HEADED INTO TOWN FOR SOME ERRANDS. ANYBODY NEEDIN' ANYTHING?"
I DIDN'T CATCH ON TO THE ROUTINE UNTIL I WAS ALMOST SEVEN. MOMMA WOULD PURSE HER LIPS AND NOT SAY NOTHING WHILE US KIDS WOULD ALL SCREAM FOR A LICORICE WHIP FROM THE DRUGSTORE.
TOBACCO
HE'D JUST SMILE LIKE HE WAS PLANNING TO RETURN BEFORE THE SUN CAME DOWN, EVEN THOUGH IT'D LIKELY BE THREE, FOUR MONTHS 'FORE WE'D SEE HIM AGAIN.
UNTIL, FINALLY, HE JUST DIDN'T COME BACK.

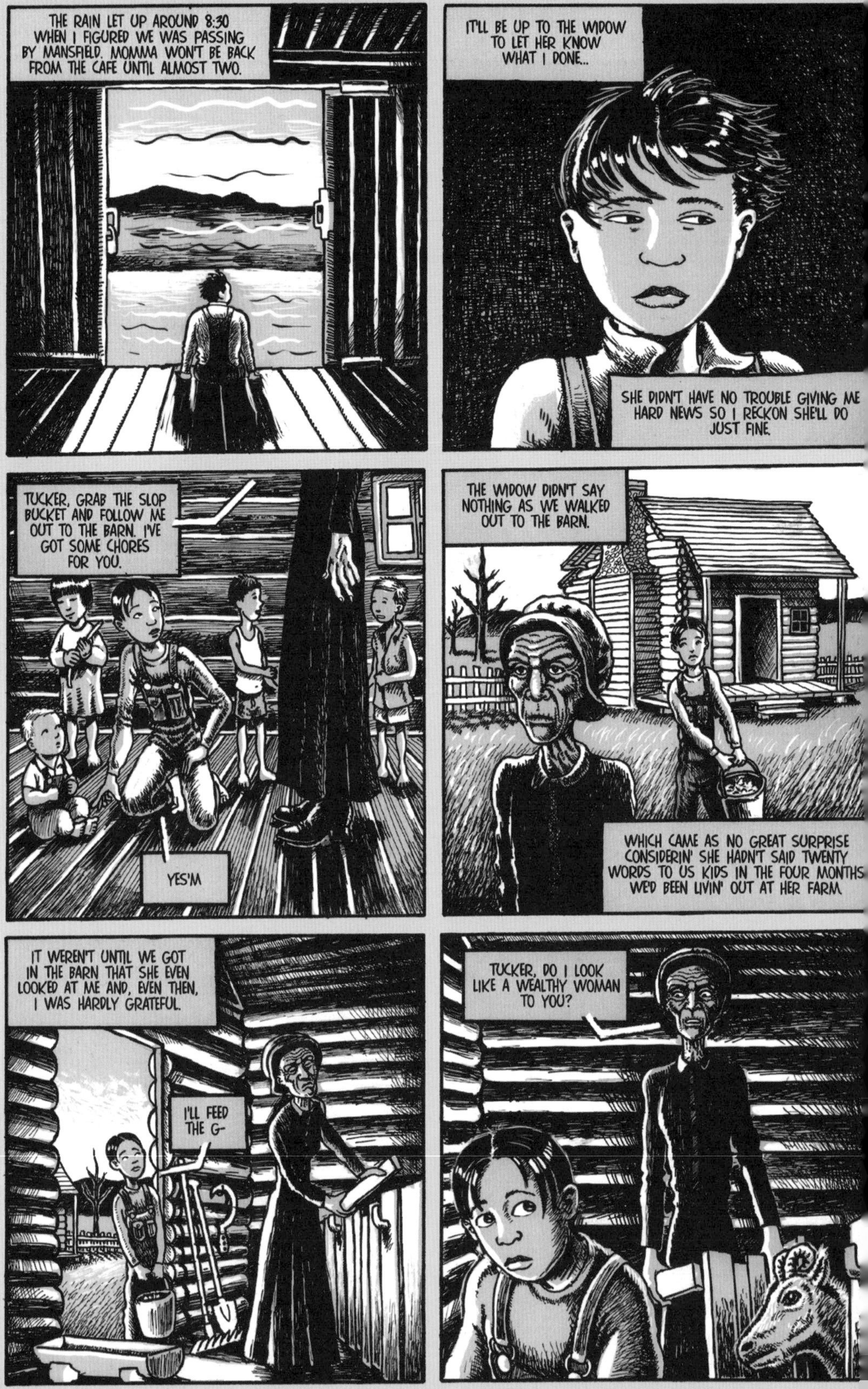
THE RAIN LET UP AROUND 8:30 WHEN I FIGURED WE WAS PASSING BY MANSFIELD. MOMMA WON'T BE BACK FROM THE CAFE UNTIL ALMOST TWO.
IT'LL BE UP TO THE WIDOW TO LET HER KNOW WHAT I DONE...
SHE DIDN'T HAVE NO TROUBLE GIVING ME HARD NEWS SO I RECKON SHE'LL DO JUST FINE.
TUCKER, GRAB THE SLOP BUCKET AND FOLLOW ME OUT TO THE BARN. I'VE GOT SOME CHORES FOR YOU.
YES'M
THE WIDOW DIDN'T SAY NOTHING AS WE WALKED OUT TO THE BARN.
WHICH CAME AS NO GREAT SURPRISE CONSIDERIN' SHE HADN'T SAID TWENTY WORDS TO US KIDS IN THE FOUR MONTHS WE'D BEEN LIVIN' OUT AT HER FARM.
IT WEREN'T UNTIL WE GOT IN THE BARN THAT SHE EVEN LOOKED AT ME AND, EVEN THEN, I WAS HARDLY GRATEFUL.
I'LL FEED THE G-
TUCKER, DO I LOOK LIKE A WEALTHY WOMAN TO YOU?

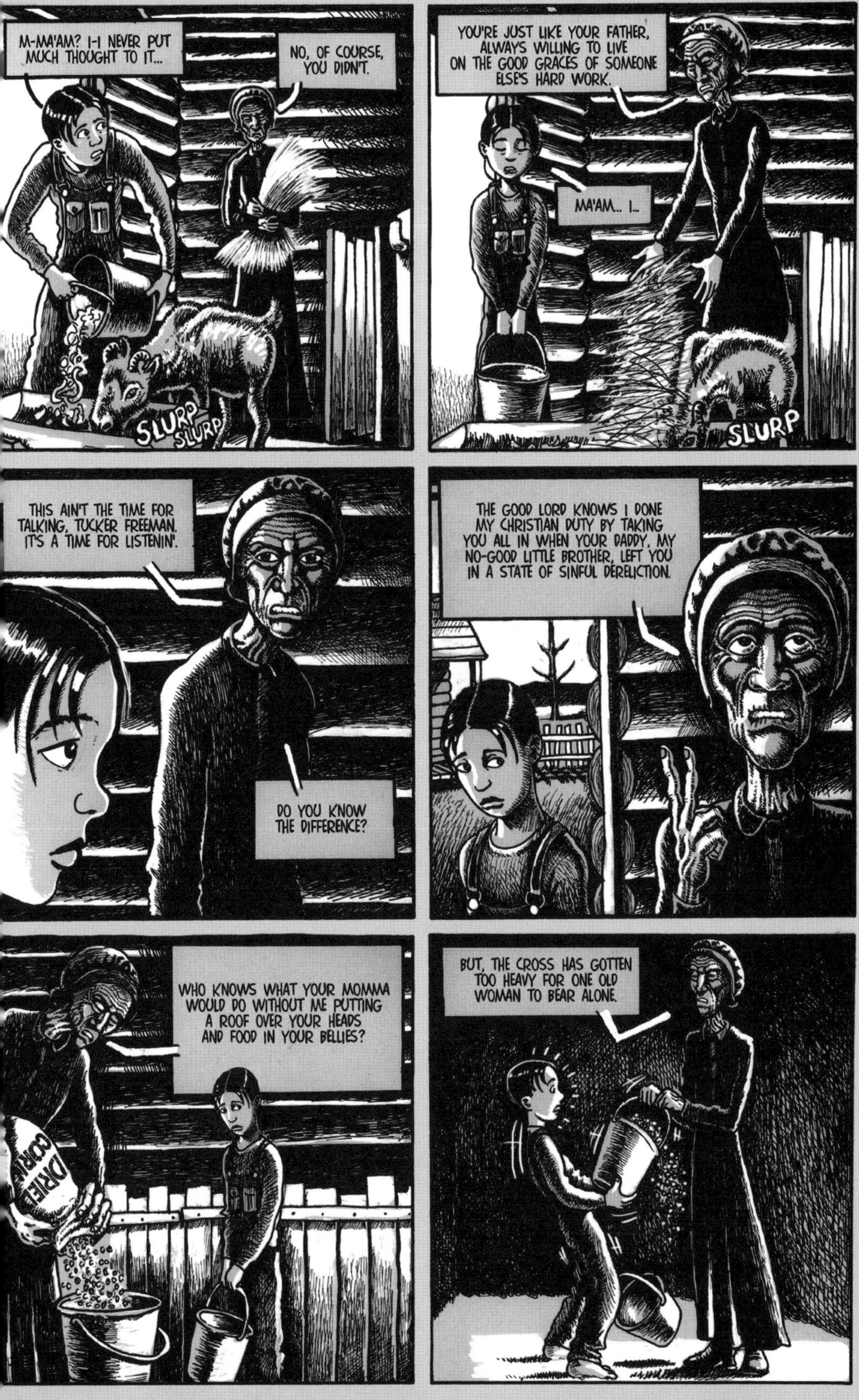
M-MA'AM? I-I NEVER PUT MUCH THOUGHT TO IT...
NO, OF COURSE, YOU DIDN'T.
SLURP SLURP
YOU'RE JUST LIKE YOUR FATHER, ALWAYS WILLING TO LIVE ON THE GOOD GRACES OF SOMEONE ELSE'S HARD WORK.
MA'AM.. I..
SLURP
THIS AIN'T THE TIME FOR TALKING, TUCKER FREEMAN. IT'S A TIME FOR LISTENIN'.
DO YOU KNOW THE DIFFERENCE?
THE GOOD LORD KNOWS I DONE MY CHRISTIAN DUTY BY TAKING YOU ALL IN WHEN YOUR DADDY, MY NO-GOOD LITTLE BROTHER, LEFT YOU IN A STATE OF SINFUL DERELICTION.
WHO KNOWS WHAT YOUR MOMMA WOULD DO WITHOUT ME PUTTING A ROOF OVER YOUR HEADS AND FOOD IN YOUR BELLIES?
DRIED CORN
BUT, THE CROSS HAS GOTTEN TOO HEAVY FOR ONE OLD WOMAN TO BEAR ALONE.

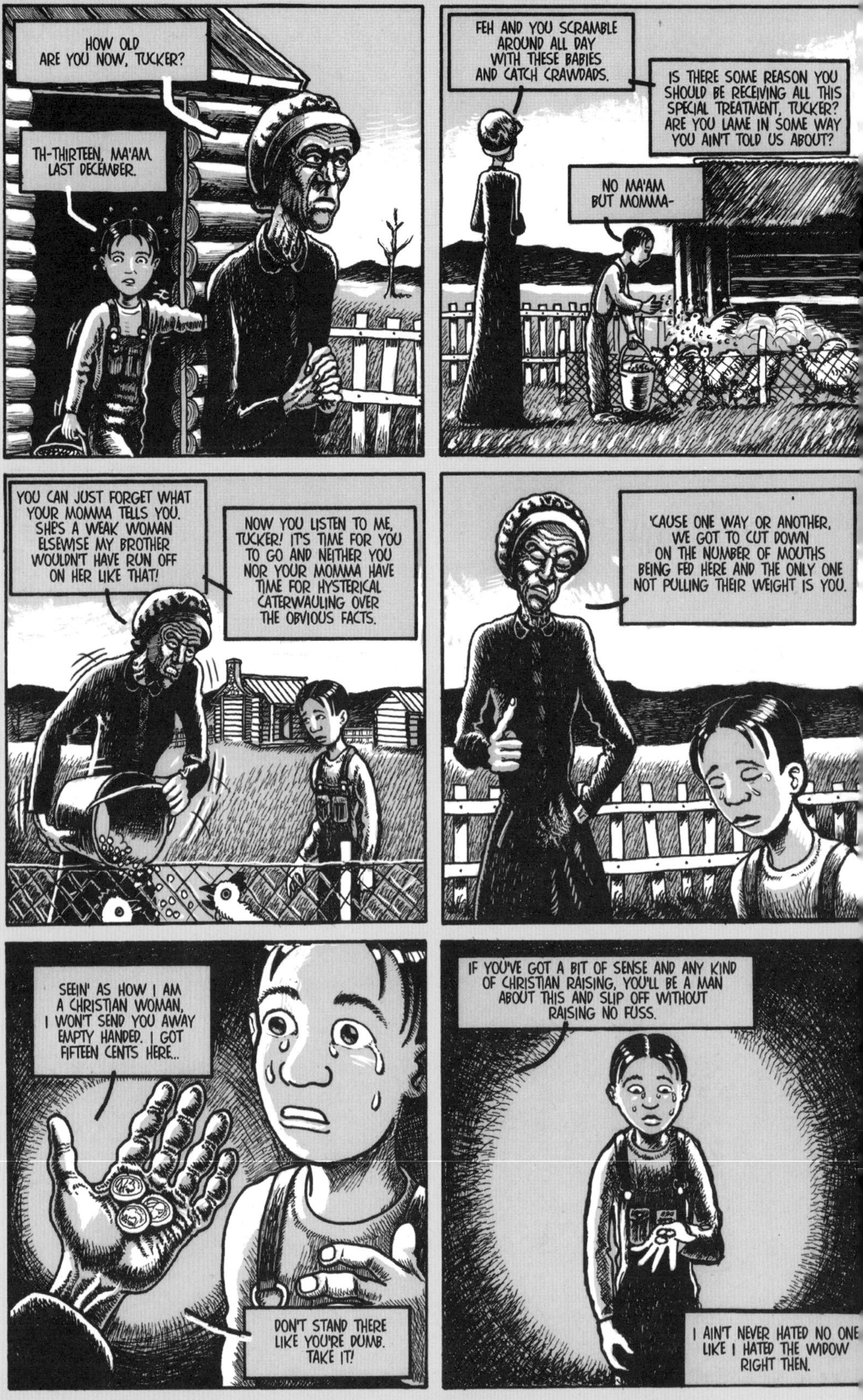
HOW OLD ARE YOU NOW, TUCKER?
TH-THIRTEEN, MA'AM. LAST DECEMBER.
FEH AND YOU SCRAMBLE AROUND ALL DAY WITH THESE BABIES AND CATCH CRAWDADS.
IS THERE SOME REASON YOU SHOULD BE RECEIVING ALL THIS SPECIAL TREATMENT, TUCKER? ARE YOU LAME IN SOME WAY YOU AIN'T TOLD US ABOUT?
NO MA'AM BUT MOMMA-
YOU CAN JUST FORGET WHAT YOUR MOMMA TELLS YOU. SHE'S A WEAK WOMAN ELSEWISE MY BROTHER WOULDN'T HAVE RUN OFF ON HER LIKE THAT!
NOW YOU LISTEN TO ME, TUCKER! IT'S TIME FOR YOU TO GO AND NEITHER YOU NOR YOUR MOMMA HAVE TIME FOR HYSTERICAL CATERWAULING OVER THE OBVIOUS FACTS.
'CAUSE ONE WAY OR ANOTHER, WE GOT TO CUT DOWN ON THE NUMBER OF MOUTHS BEING FED HERE AND THE ONLY ONE NOT PULLING THEIR WEIGHT IS YOU.
SEEIN' AS HOW I AM A CHRISTIAN WOMAN, I WON'T SEND YOU AWAY EMPTY HANDED. I GOT FIFTEEN CENTS HERE...
DON'T STAND THERE LIKE YOU'RE DUMB. TAKE IT!
IF YOU'VE GOT A BIT OF SENSE AND ANY KIND OF CHRISTIAN RAISING, YOU'LL BE A MAN ABOUT THIS AND SLIP OFF WITHOUT RAISING NO FUSS.
I AIN'T NEVER HATED NO ONE LIKE I HATED THE WIDOW RIGHT THEN.

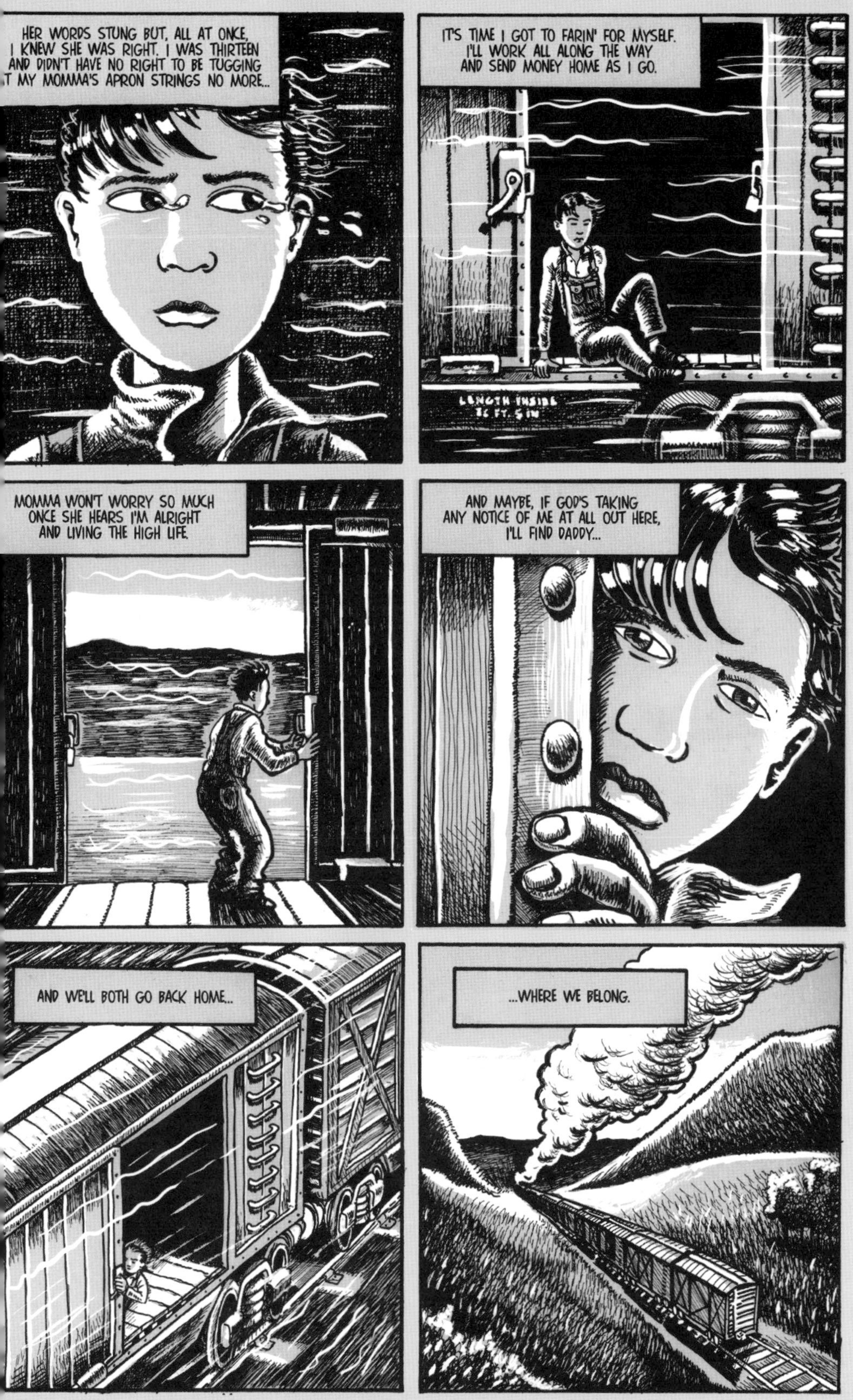
HER WORDS STUNG BUT, ALL AT ONCE, I KNEW SHE WAS RIGHT. I WAS THIRTEEN AND DIDN'T HAVE NO RIGHT TO BE TUGGING AT MY MOMMA'S APRON STRINGS NO MORE...
IT'S TIME I GOT TO FARIN' FOR MYSELF. I'LL WORK ALL ALONG THE WAY AND SEND MONEY HOME AS I GO.
LENGTH INSIDE
36 FT. 5 IN
MOMMA WON'T WORRY SO MUCH ONCE SHE HEARS I'M ALRIGHT AND LIVING THE HIGH LIFE.
AND MAYBE, IF GOD'S TAKING ANY NOTICE OF ME AT ALL OUT HERE, I'LL FIND DADDY...
AND WE'LL BOTH GO BACK HOME...
...WHERE WE BELONG.

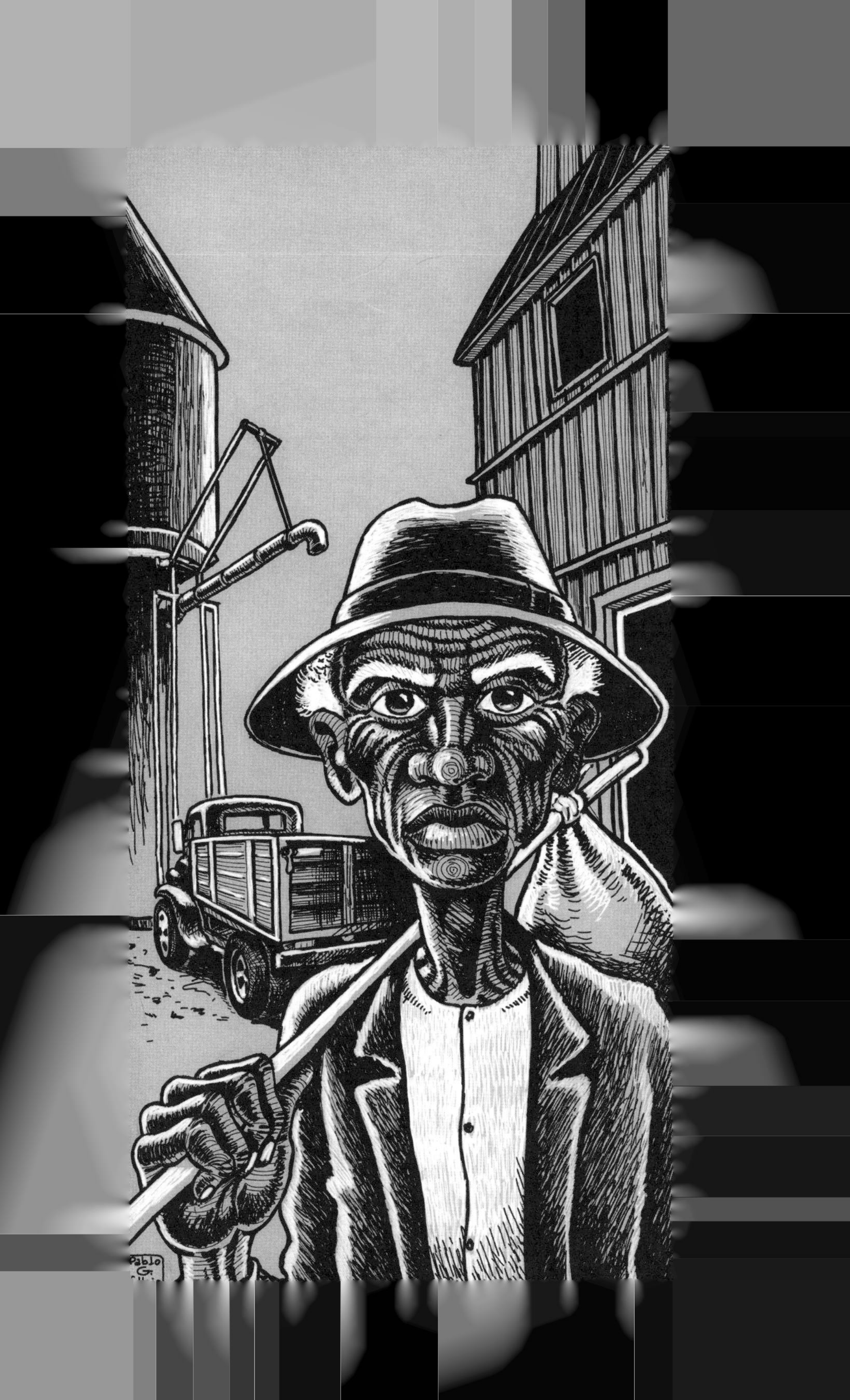
Pablo G.

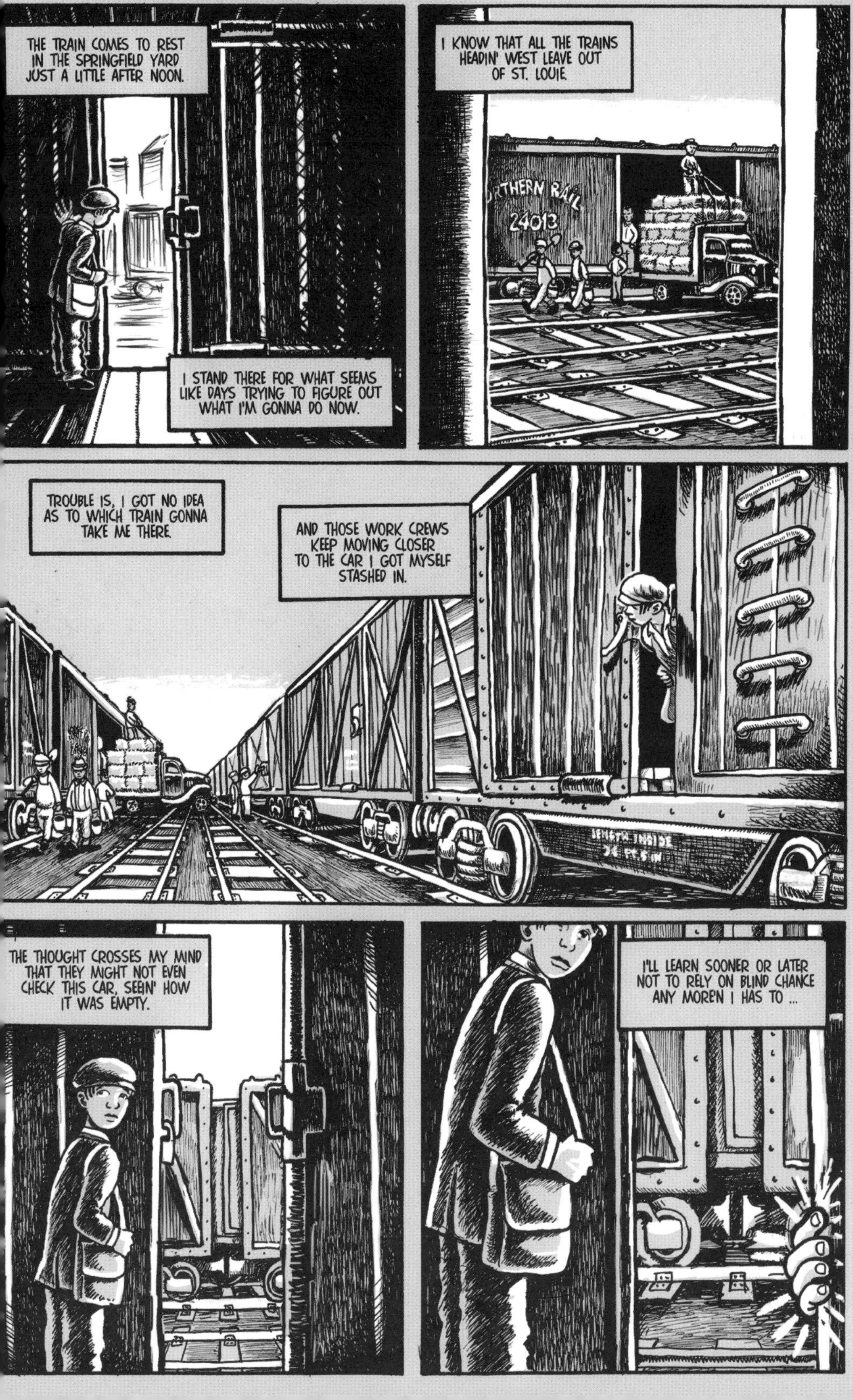
THE TRAIN COMES TO REST IN THE SPRINGFIELD YARD JUST A LITTLE AFTER NOON.
I STAND THERE FOR WHAT SEEMS LIKE DAYS TRYING TO FIGURE OUT WHAT I'M GONNA DO NOW.
I KNOW THAT ALL THE TRAINS HEADIN' WEST LEAVE OUT OF ST. LOUIE.
RTHERN RAIL
24013
TROUBLE IS, I GOT NO IDEA AS TO WHICH TRAIN GONNA TAKE ME THERE.
AND THOSE WORK CREWS KEEP MOVING CLOSER TO THE CAR I GOT MYSELF STASHED IN.
THE THOUGHT CROSSES MY MIND THAT THEY MIGHT NOT EVEN CHECK THIS CAR, SEEIN' HOW IT WAS EMPTY.
I'LL LEARN SOONER OR LATER NOT TO RELY ON BLIND CHANCE ANY MOREN I HAS TO ...

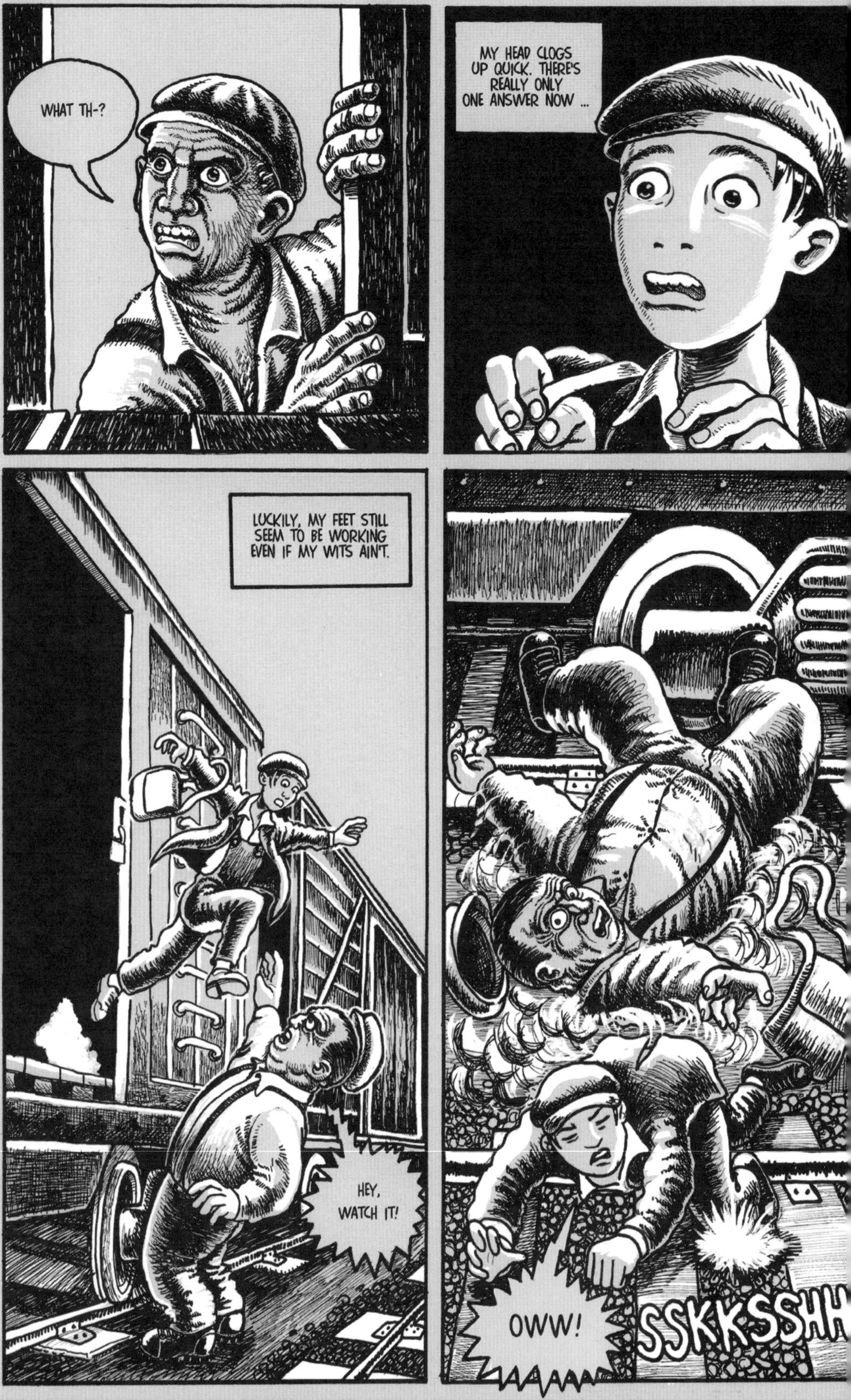
WHAT TH-?
MY HEAD CLOGS UP QUICK. THERE'S REALLY ONLY ONE ANSWER NOW ...
LUCKILY, MY FEET STILL SEEM TO BE WORKING EVEN IF MY WITS AIN'T.
HEY, WATCH IT!
OWW!
SSKKSSHH

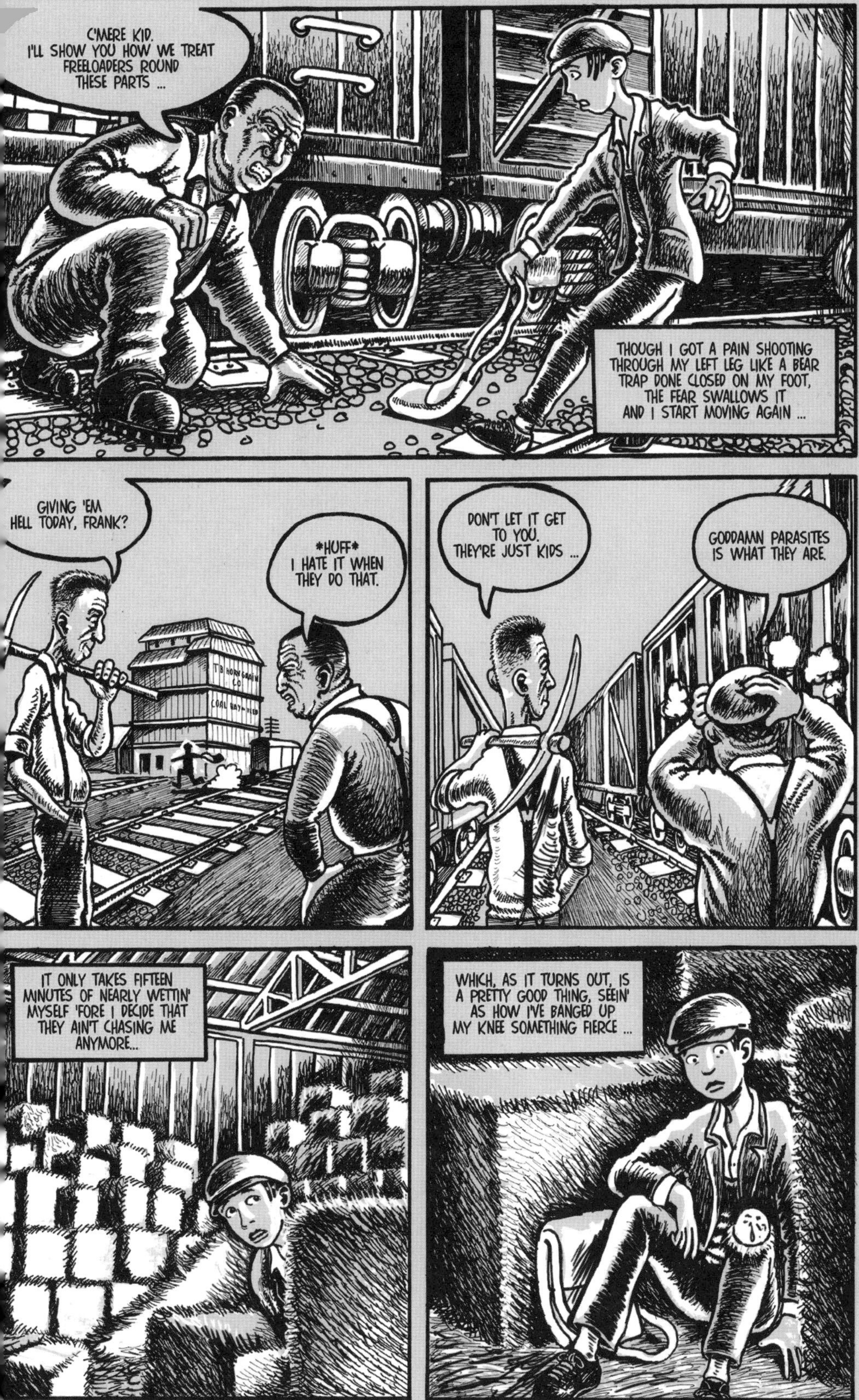
C'MERE KID. I'LL SHOW YOU HOW WE TREAT FREELOADERS ROUND THESE PARTS ...
THOUGH I GOT A PAIN SHOOTING THROUGH MY LEFT LEG LIKE A BEAR TRAP DONE CLOSED ON MY FOOT, THE FEAR SWALLOWS IT AND I START MOVING AGAIN ...
GIVING 'EM HELL TODAY, FRANK?
HUFF I HATE IT WHEN THEY DO THAT.
DON'T LET IT GET TO YOU. THEY'RE JUST KIDS ...
GODDAMN PARASITES IS WHAT THEY ARE.
IT ONLY TAKES FIFTEEN MINUTES OF NEARLY WETTIN' MYSELF 'FORE I DECIDE THAT THEY AIN'T CHASING ME ANYMORE...
WHICH, AS IT TURNS OUT, IS A PRETTY GOOD THING, SEEIN' AS HOW I'VE BANGED UP MY KNEE SOMETHING FIERCE ...

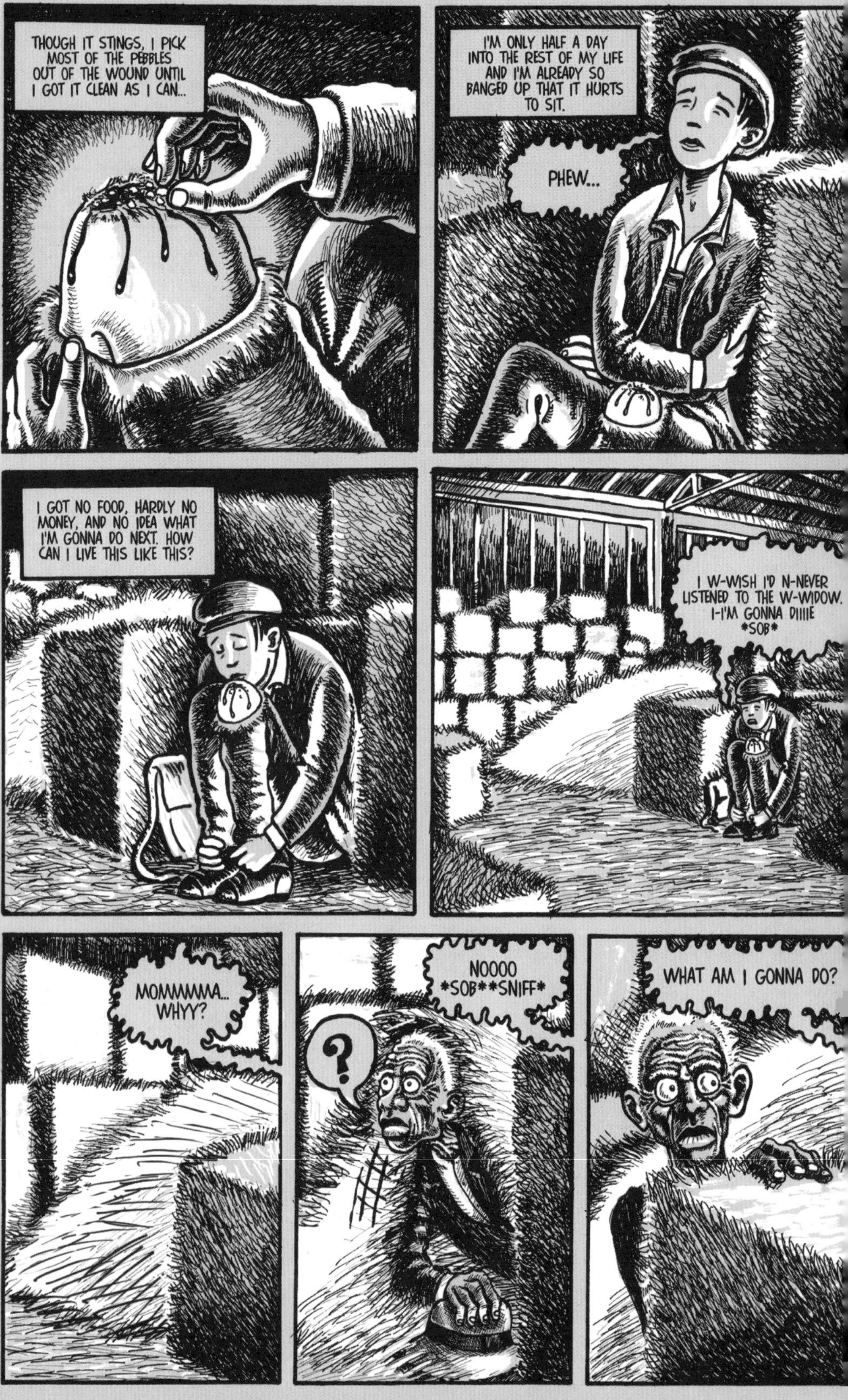
THOUGH IT STINGS, I PICK MOST OF THE PEBBLES OUT OF THE WOUND UNTIL I GOT IT CLEAN AS I CAN...
I'M ONLY HALF A DAY INTO THE REST OF MY LIFE AND I'M ALREADY SO BANGED UP THAT IT HURTS TO SIT.
PHEW...
I GOT NO FOOD, HARDLY NO MONEY, AND NO IDEA WHAT I'M GONNA DO NEXT. HOW CAN I LIVE THIS LIKE THIS?
I W-WISH I'D N-NEVER LISTENED TO THE W-WIDOW. I-I'M GONNA DIIIIE *SOB*
MOMMMMA... WHYY?
NOOOO *SOB**SNIFF*
?
WHAT AM I GONNA DO?

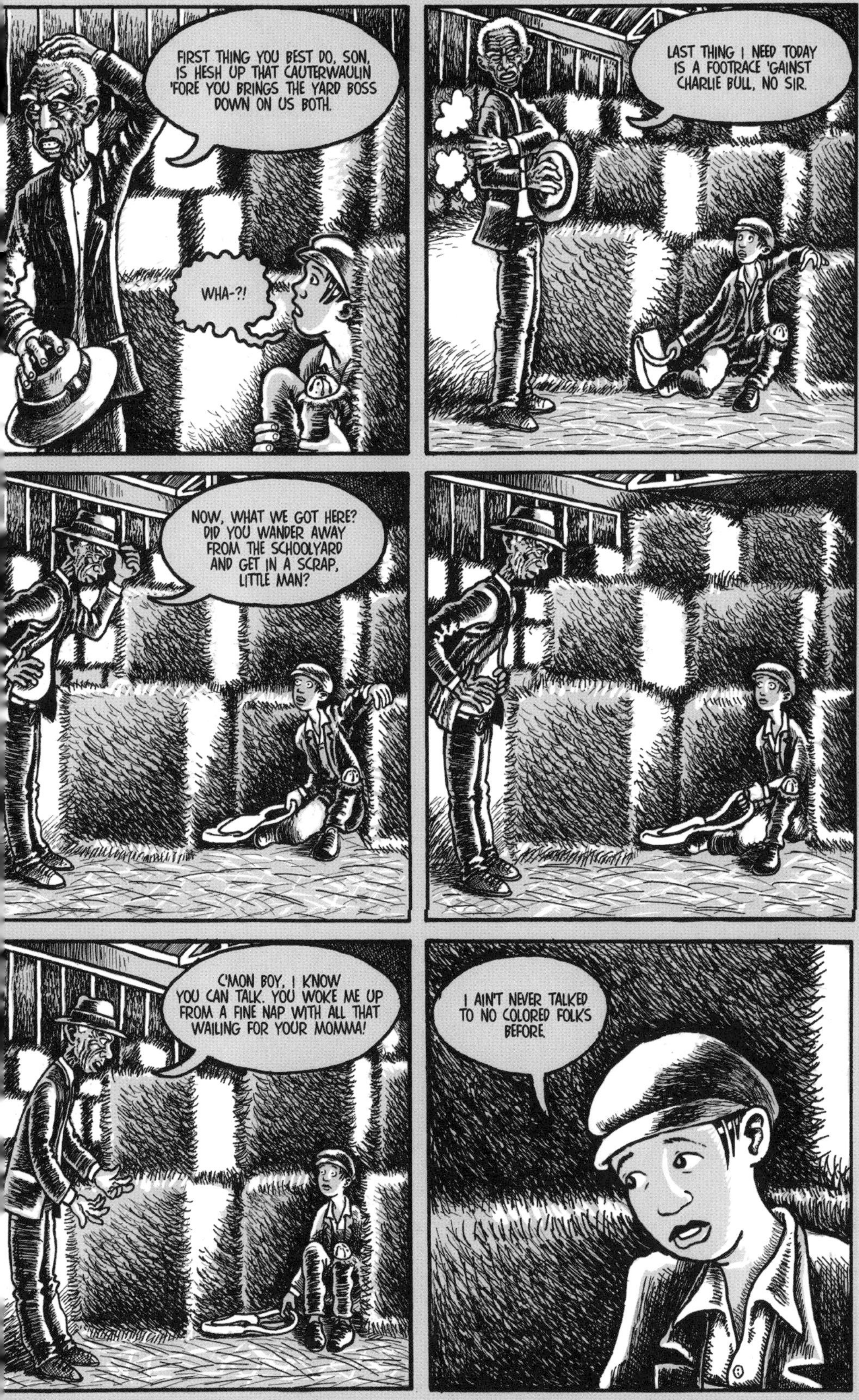
FIRST THING YOU BEST DO, SON, IS HESH UP THAT CAUTERWAULIN 'FORE YOU BRINGS THE YARD BOSS DOWN ON US BOTH.
WHA-?!
LAST THING I NEED TODAY IS A FOOTRACE 'GAINST CHARLIE BULL, NO SIR.
NOW, WHAT WE GOT HERE? DID YOU WANDER AWAY FROM THE SCHOOLYARD AND GET IN A SCRAP, LITTLE MAN?
C'MON BOY, I KNOW YOU CAN TALK. YOU WOKE ME UP FROM A FINE NAP WITH ALL THAT WAILING FOR YOUR MOMMA!
I AIN'T NEVER TALKED TO NO COLORED FOLKS BEFORE.

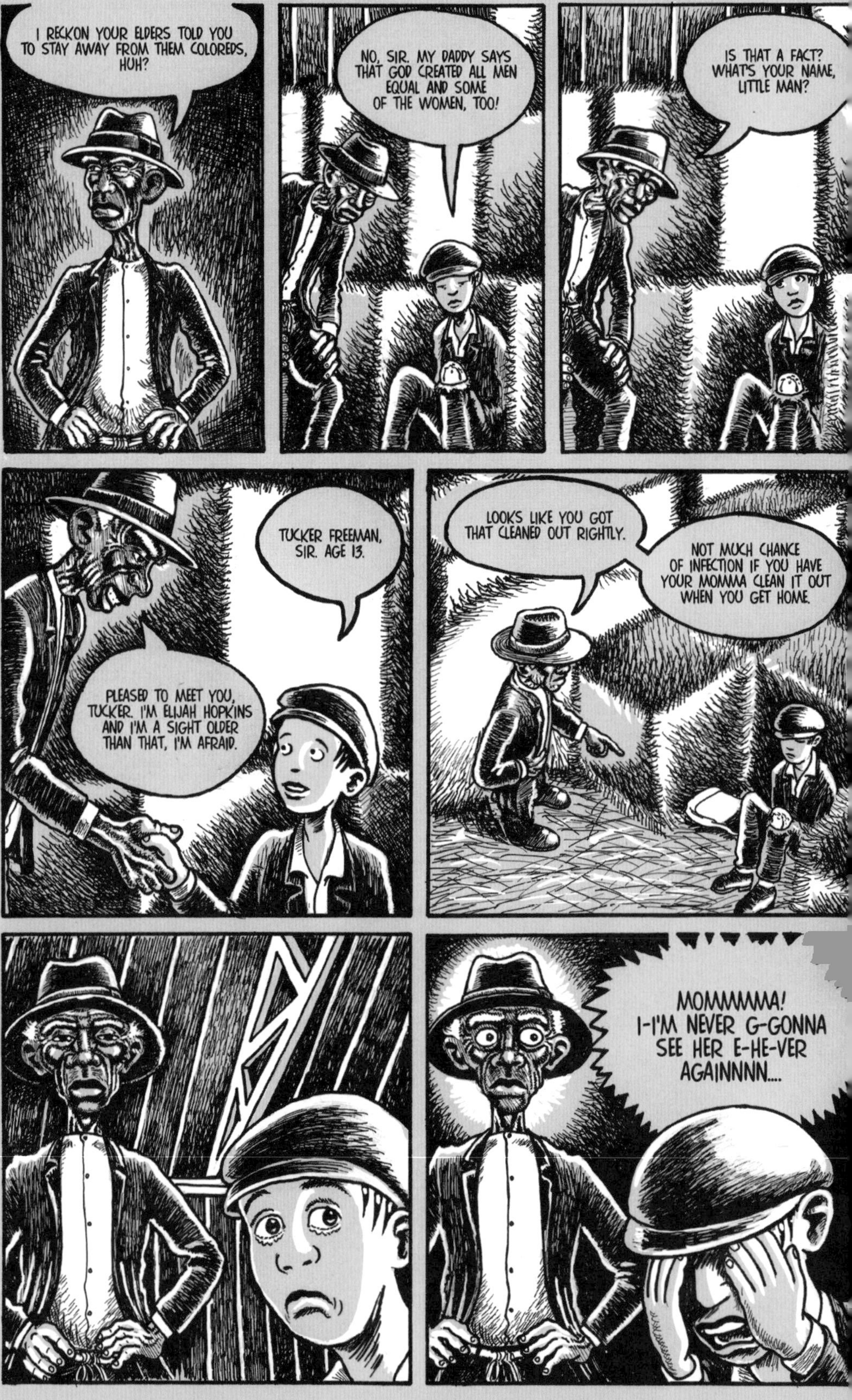
I RECKON YOUR ELDERS TOLD YOU TO STAY AWAY FROM THEM COLOREDS, HUH?
NO, SIR. MY DADDY SAYS THAT GOD CREATED ALL MEN EQUAL AND SOME OF THE WOMEN, TOO!
IS THAT A FACT? WHAT'S YOUR NAME, LITTLE MAN?
TUCKER FREEMAN, SIR. AGE 13.
PLEASED TO MEET YOU, TUCKER. I'M ELIJAH HOPKINS AND I'M A SIGHT OLDER THAN THAT, I'M AFRAID.
LOOKS LIKE YOU GOT THAT CLEANED OUT RIGHTLY.
NOT MUCH CHANCE OF INFECTION IF YOU HAVE YOUR MOMMA CLEAN IT OUT WHEN YOU GET HOME.
MOMMMMMA! I-I'M NEVER G-GONNA SEE HER E-HE-VER AGAINNNN....

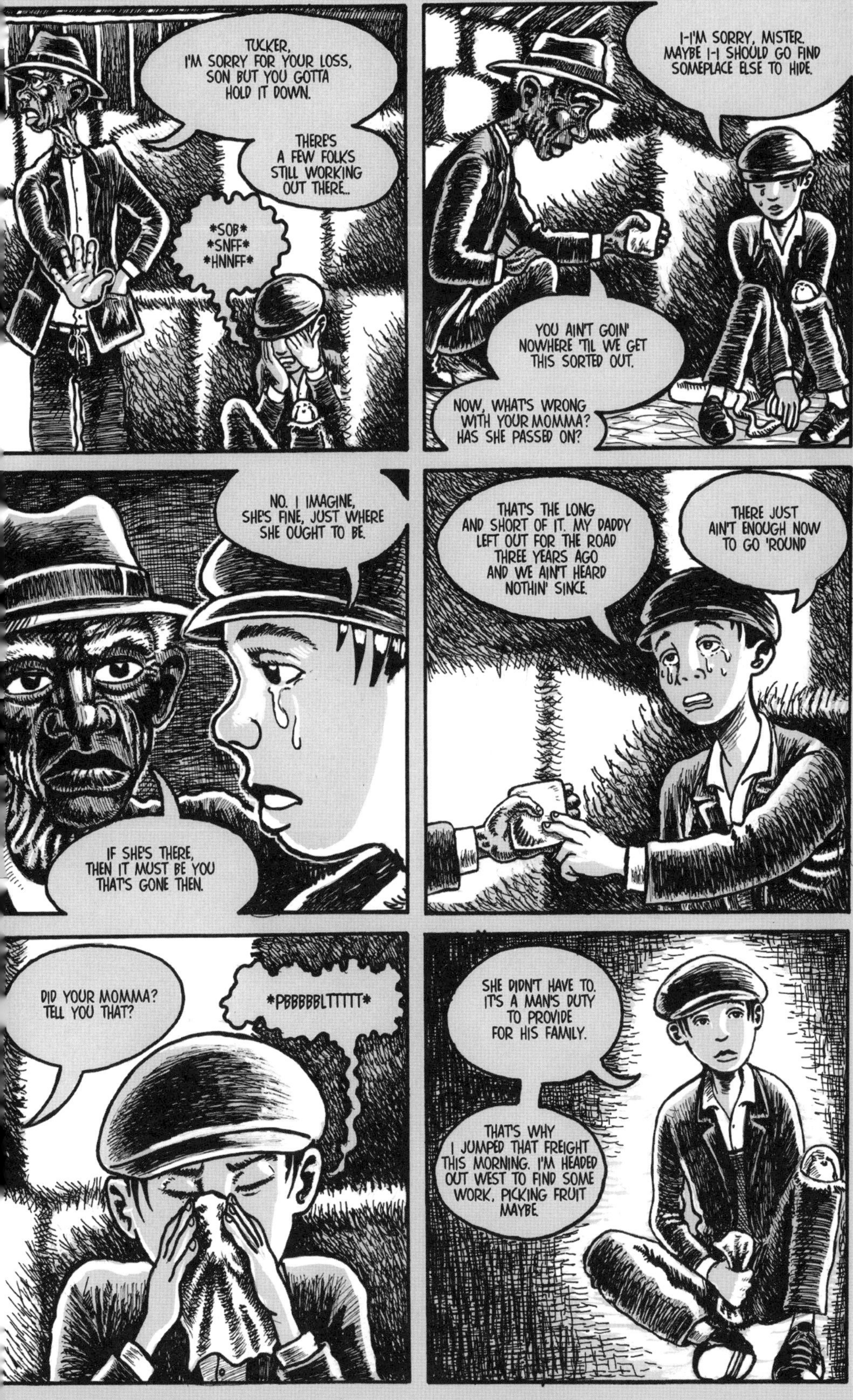
TUCKER,
I'M SORRY FOR YOUR LOSS, SON BUT YOU GOTTA HOLD IT DOWN.
THERE'S A FEW FOLKS STILL WORKING OUT THERE..
SOB *SNFF* *HNNFF*
I-I'M SORRY, MISTER. MAYBE I-I SHOULD GO FIND SOMEPLACE ELSE TO HIDE.
YOU AIN'T GOIN' NOWHERE 'TIL WE GET THIS SORTED OUT.
NOW, WHAT'S WRONG WITH YOUR MOMMA? HAS SHE PASSED ON?
NO. I IMAGINE, SHE'S FINE, JUST WHERE SHE OUGHT TO BE.
IF SHE'S THERE, THEN IT MUST BE YOU THAT'S GONE THEN.
THAT'S THE LONG AND SHORT OF IT. MY DADDY LEFT OUT FOR THE ROAD THREE YEARS AGO AND WE AIN'T HEARD NOTHIN' SINCE.
THERE JUST AIN'T ENOUGH NOW TO GO 'ROUND
DID YOUR MOMMA? TELL YOU THAT?
PBBBBBLTTTTT
SHE DIDN'T HAVE TO. IT'S A MAN'S DUTY TO PROVIDE FOR HIS FAMILY.
THAT'S WHY I JUMPED THAT FREIGHT THIS MORNING. I'M HEADED OUT WEST TO FIND SOME WORK, PICKING FRUIT MAYBE.

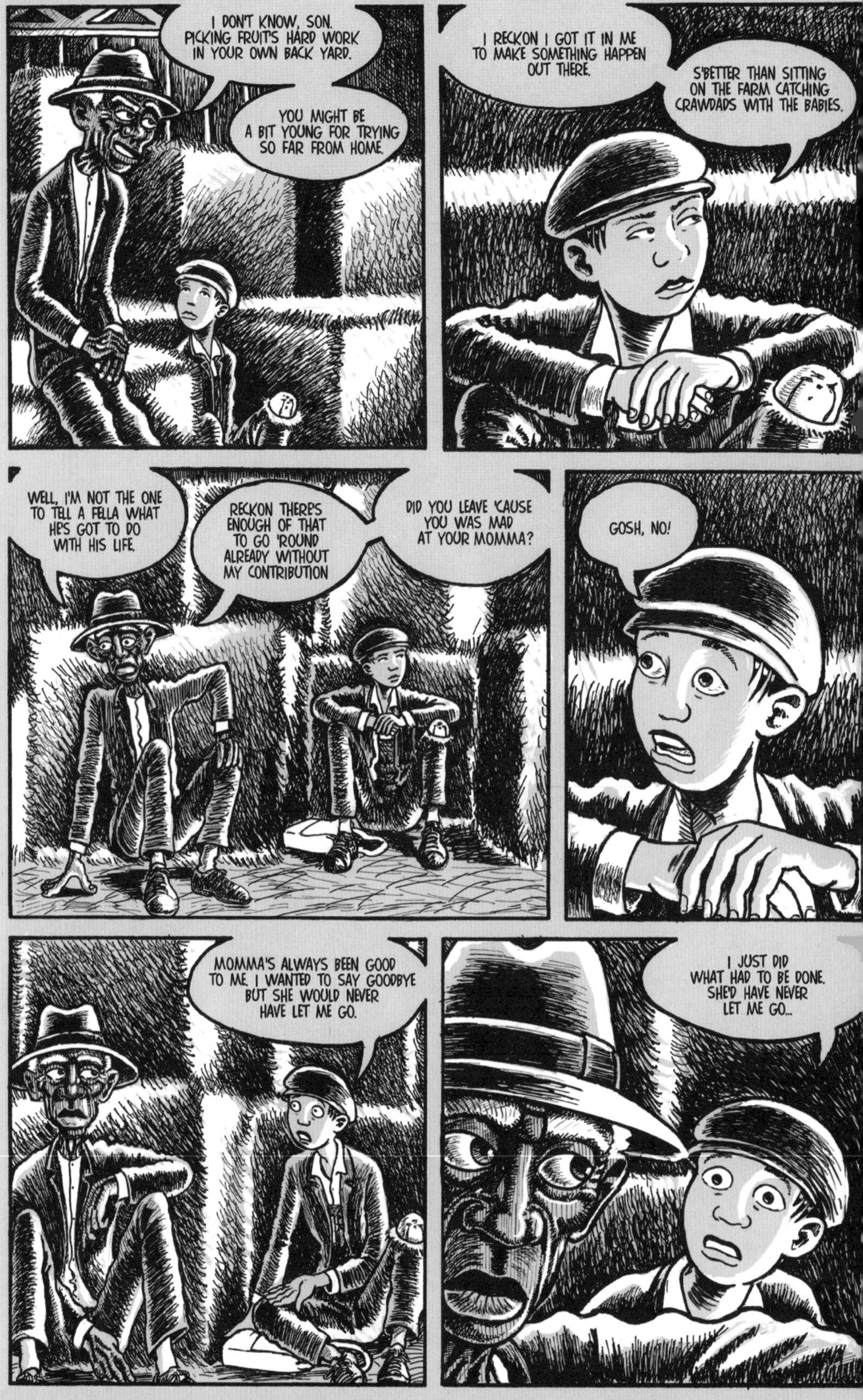
I DON'T KNOW, SON. PICKING FRUIT'S HARD WORK IN YOUR OWN BACK YARD.
YOU MIGHT BE A BIT YOUNG FOR TRYING SO FAR FROM HOME.
I RECKON I GOT IT IN ME TO MAKE SOMETHING HAPPEN OUT THERE.
S'BETTER THAN SITTING ON THE FARM CATCHING CRAWDADS WITH THE BABIES.
WELL, I'M NOT THE ONE TO TELL A FELLA WHAT HE'S GOT TO DO WITH HIS LIFE.
RECKON THERE'S ENOUGH OF THAT TO GO 'ROUND ALREADY WITHOUT MY CONTRIBUTION
DID YOU LEAVE 'CAUSE YOU WAS MAD AT YOUR MOMMA?
GOSH, NO!
MOMMA'S ALWAYS BEEN GOOD TO ME. I WANTED TO SAY GOODBYE BUT SHE WOULD NEVER HAVE LET ME GO.
I JUST DID WHAT HAD TO BE DONE. SHE'D HAVE NEVER LET ME GO...

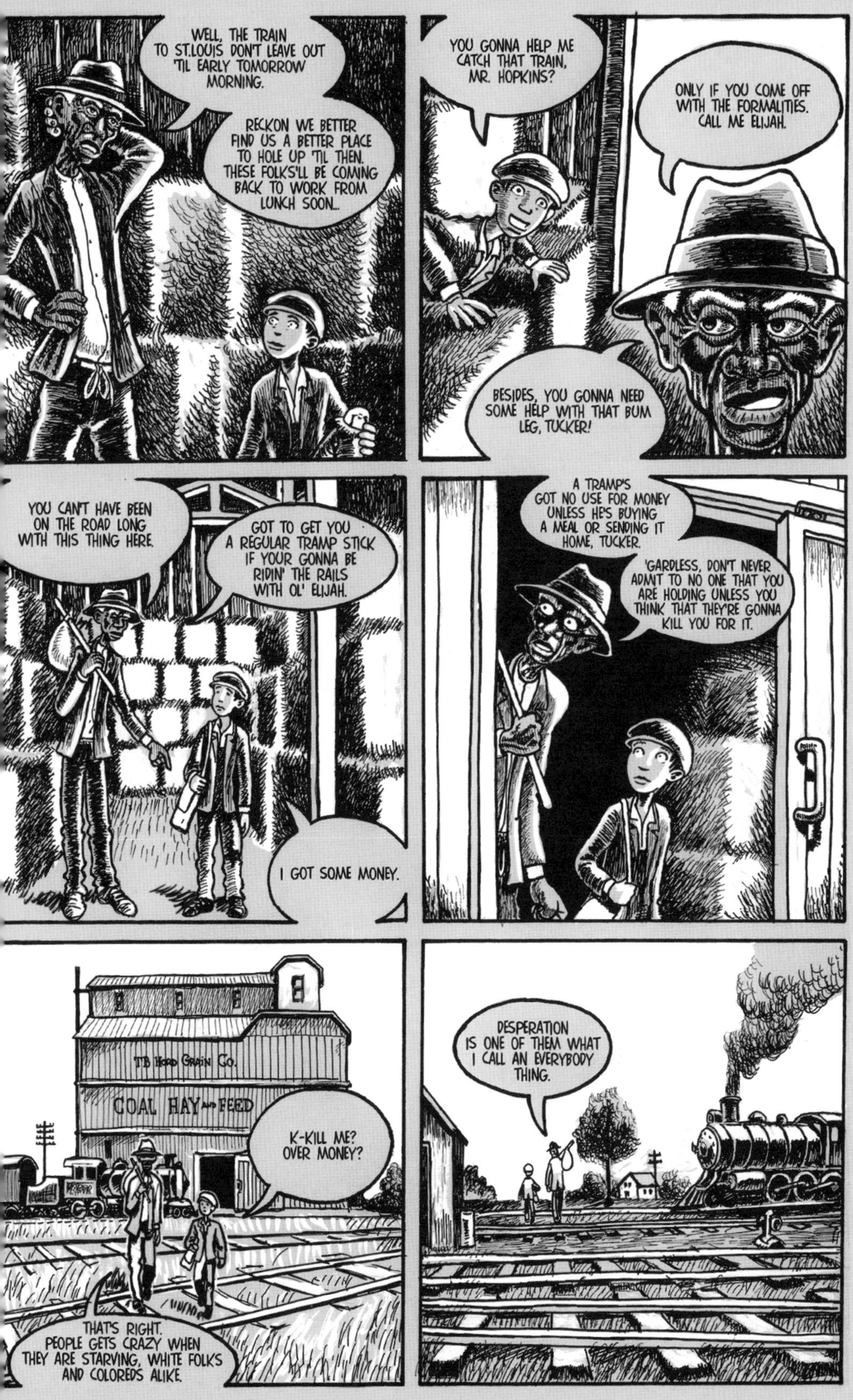
WELL, THE TRAIN TO ST.LOUIS DON'T LEAVE OUT 'TIL EARLY TOMORROW MORNING.
RECKON WE BETTER FIND US A BETTER PLACE TO HOLE UP 'TIL THEN. THESE FOLK'S'LL BE COMING BACK TO WORK FROM LUNCH SOON..
YOU GONNA HELP ME CATCH THAT TRAIN, MR. HOPKINS?
ONLY IF YOU COME OFF WITH THE FORMALITIES. CALL ME ELIJAH.
BESIDES, YOU GONNA NEED SOME HELP WITH THAT BUM LEG, TUCKER!
YOU CAN'T HAVE BEEN ON THE ROAD LONG WITH THIS THING HERE.
GOT TO GET YOU A REGULAR TRAMP STICK IF YOUR GONNA BE RIDIN' THE RAILS WITH OL' ELIJAH.
I GOT SOME MONEY.
A TRAMP'S GOT NO USE FOR MONEY UNLESS HE'S BUYING A MEAL OR SENDING IT HOME, TUCKER.
'GARDLESS, DON'T NEVER ADMIT TO NO ONE THAT YOU ARE HOLDING UNLESS YOU THINK THAT THEY'RE GONNA KILL YOU FOR IT.
TB HORD GRAIN CO.
COAL HAY AND FEED
K-KILL ME? OVER MONEY?
THAT'S RIGHT. PEOPLE GETS CRAZY WHEN THEY ARE STARVING, WHITE FOLKS AND COLOREDS ALIKE.
DESPERATION IS ONE OF THEM WHAT I CALL AN EVERYBODY THING.

Chapter 3

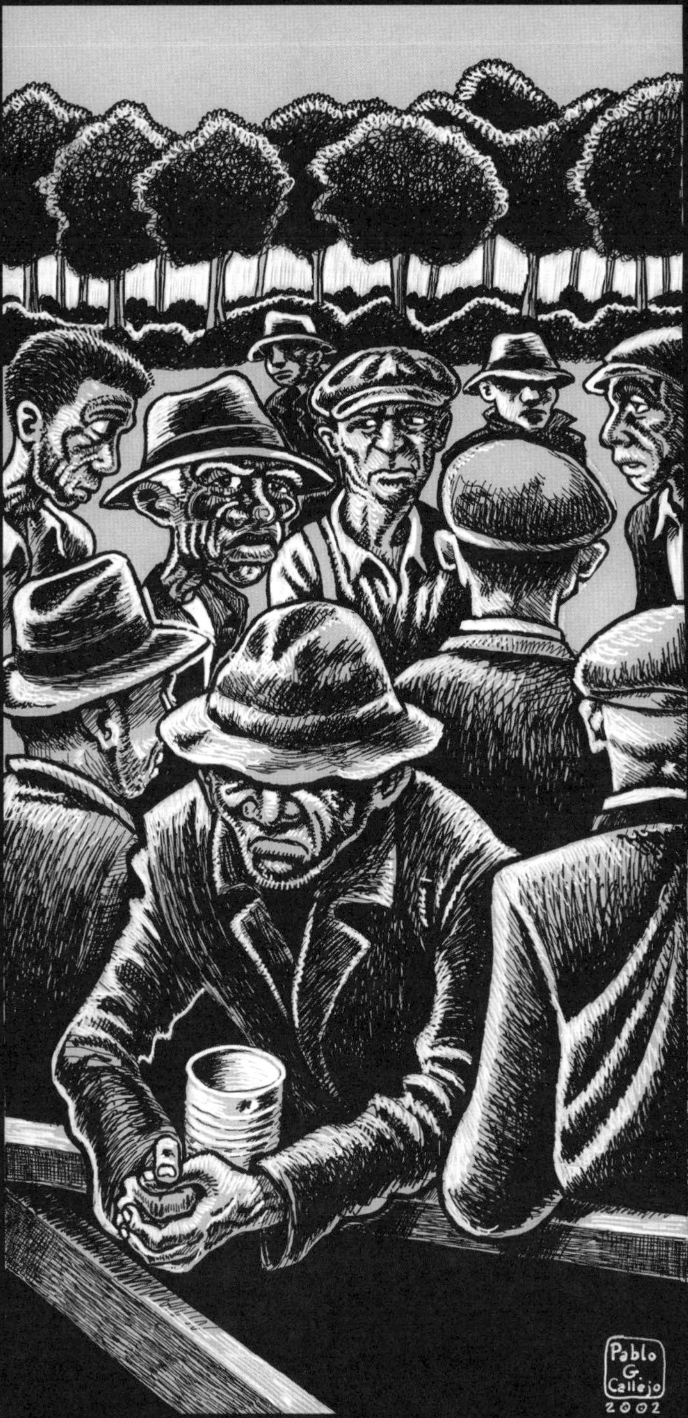
Pablo G. Callejo 2002

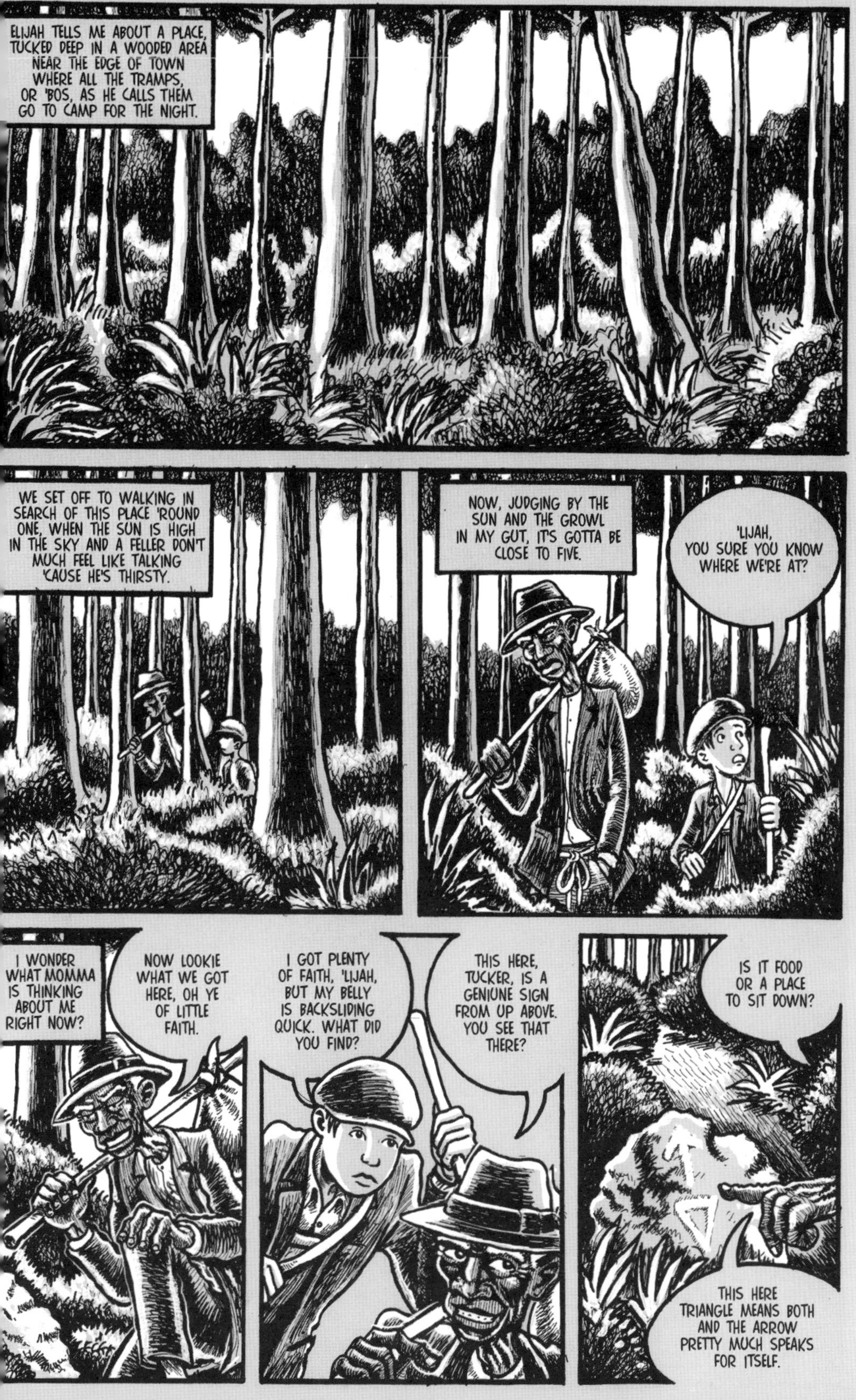
ELIJAH TELLS ME ABOUT A PLACE, TUCKED DEEP IN A WOODED AREA NEAR THE EDGE OF TOWN WHERE ALL THE TRAMPS, OR 'BOS, AS HE CALLS THEM GO TO CAMP FOR THE NIGHT.
WE SET OFF TO WALKING IN SEARCH OF THIS PLACE 'ROUND ONE, WHEN THE SUN IS HIGH IN THE SKY AND A FELLER DON'T MUCH FEEL LIKE TALKING 'CAUSE HE'S THIRSTY.
NOW, JUDGING BY THE SUN AND THE GROWL IN MY GUT, IT'S GOTTA BE CLOSE TO FIVE.
'LIJAH, YOU SURE YOU KNOW WHERE WE'RE AT?
I WONDER WHAT MOMMA IS THINKING ABOUT ME RIGHT NOW?
NOW LOOKIE WHAT WE GOT HERE, OH YE OF LITTLE FAITH.
I GOT PLENTY OF FAITH, 'LIJAH, BUT MY BELLY IS BACKSLIDING QUICK. WHAT DID YOU FIND?
THIS HERE, TUCKER, IS A GENIUNE SIGN FROM UP ABOVE. YOU SEE THAT THERE?
IS IT FOOD OR A PLACE TO SIT DOWN?
THIS HERE TRIANGLE MEANS BOTH AND THE ARROW PRETTY MUCH SPEAKS FOR ITSELF.

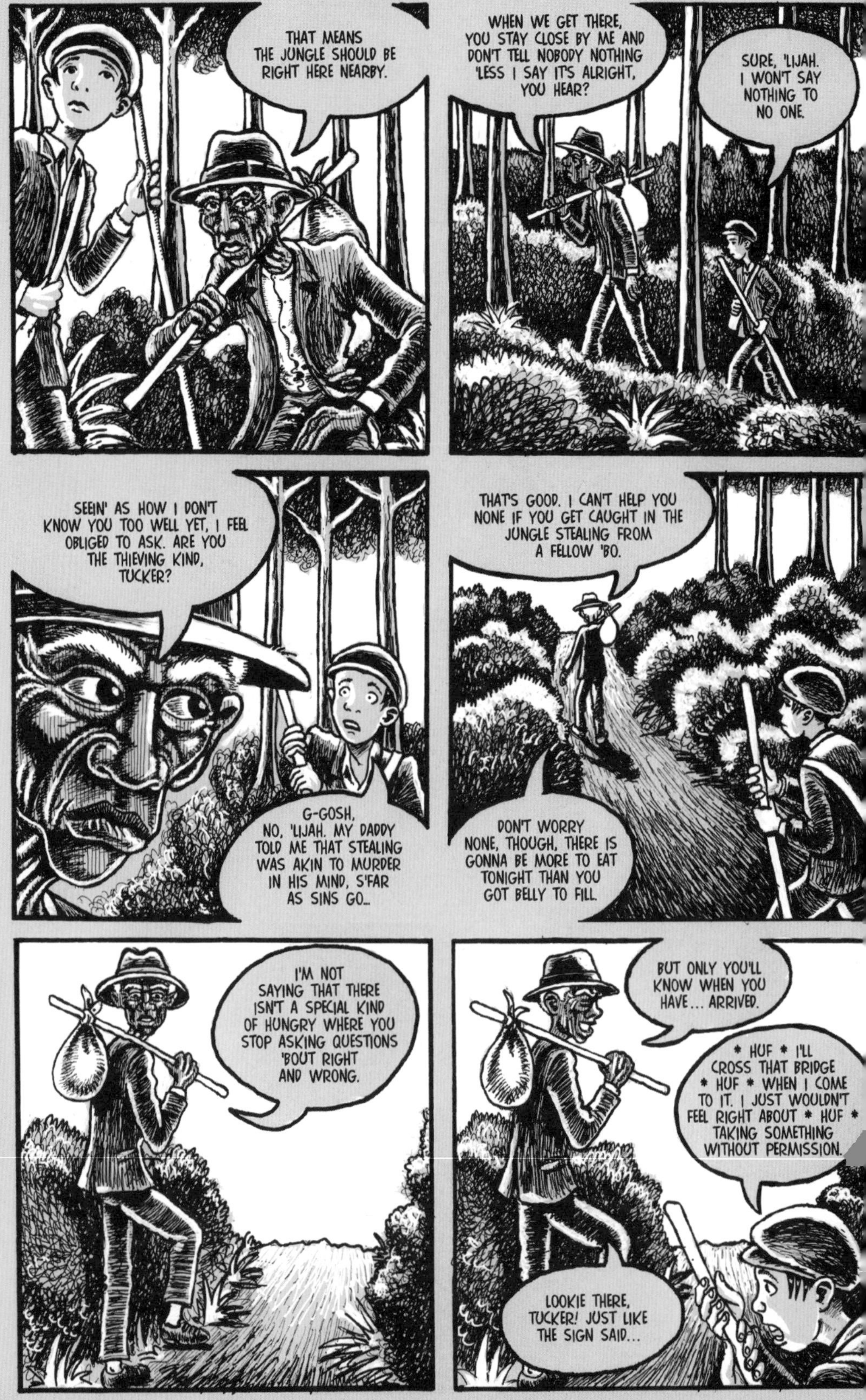
THAT MEANS THE JUNGLE SHOULD BE RIGHT HERE NEARBY.
WHEN WE GET THERE, YOU STAY CLOSE BY ME AND DON'T TELL NOBODY NOTHING 'LESS I SAY IT'S ALRIGHT, YOU HEAR?
SURE, 'LIJAH. I WON'T SAY NOTHING TO NO ONE.
SEEIN' AS HOW I DON'T KNOW YOU TOO WELL YET, I FEEL OBLIGED TO ASK. ARE YOU THE THIEVING KIND, TUCKER?
G-GOSH, NO, 'LIJAH. MY DADDY TOLD ME THAT STEALING WAS AKIN TO MURDER IN HIS MIND, S'FAR AS SINS GO...
THAT'S GOOD. I CAN'T HELP YOU NONE IF YOU GET CAUGHT IN THE JUNGLE STEALING FROM A FELLOW 'BO.
DON'T WORRY NONE, THOUGH, THERE IS GONNA BE MORE TO EAT TONIGHT THAN YOU GOT BELLY TO FILL.
I'M NOT SAYING THAT THERE ISN'T A SPECIAL KIND OF HUNGRY WHERE YOU STOP ASKING QUESTIONS 'BOUT RIGHT AND WRONG.
BUT ONLY YOU'LL KNOW WHEN YOU HAVE... ARRIVED.
* HUF * I'LL CROSS THAT BRIDGE * HUF * WHEN I COME TO IT. I JUST WOULDN'T FEEL RIGHT ABOUT * HUF * TAKING SOMETHING WITHOUT PERMISSION.
LOOKIE THERE, TUCKER! JUST LIKE THE SIGN SAID...

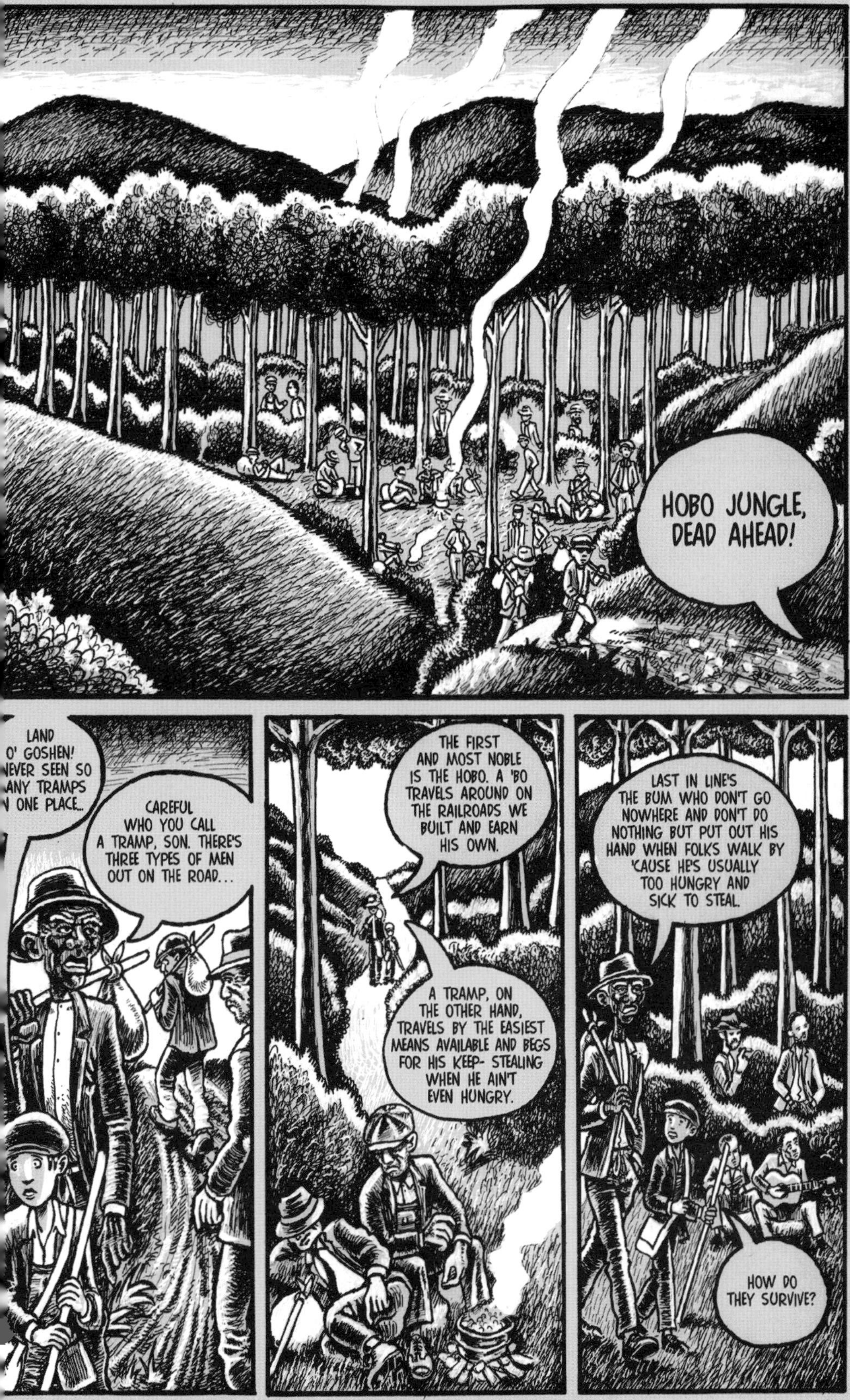
HOBO JUNGLE, DEAD AHEAD!
LAND O' GOSHEN! NEVER SEEN SO ANY TRAMPS N ONE PLACE..
CAREFUL WHO YOU CALL A TRAMP, SON. THERE'S THREE TYPES OF MEN OUT ON THE ROAD...
THE FIRST AND MOST NOBLE IS THE HOBO. A 'BO TRAVELS AROUND ON THE RAILROADS WE BUILT AND EARN HIS OWN.
A TRAMP, ON THE OTHER HAND, TRAVELS BY THE EASIEST MEANS AVAILABLE AND BEGS FOR HIS KEEP- STEALING WHEN HE AIN'T EVEN HUNGRY.
LAST IN LINE'S THE BUM WHO DON'T GO NOWHERE AND DON'T DO NOTHING BUT PUT OUT HIS HAND WHEN FOLKS WALK BY 'CAUSE HE'S USUALLY TOO HUNGRY AND SICK TO STEAL.
HOW DO THEY SURVIVE?

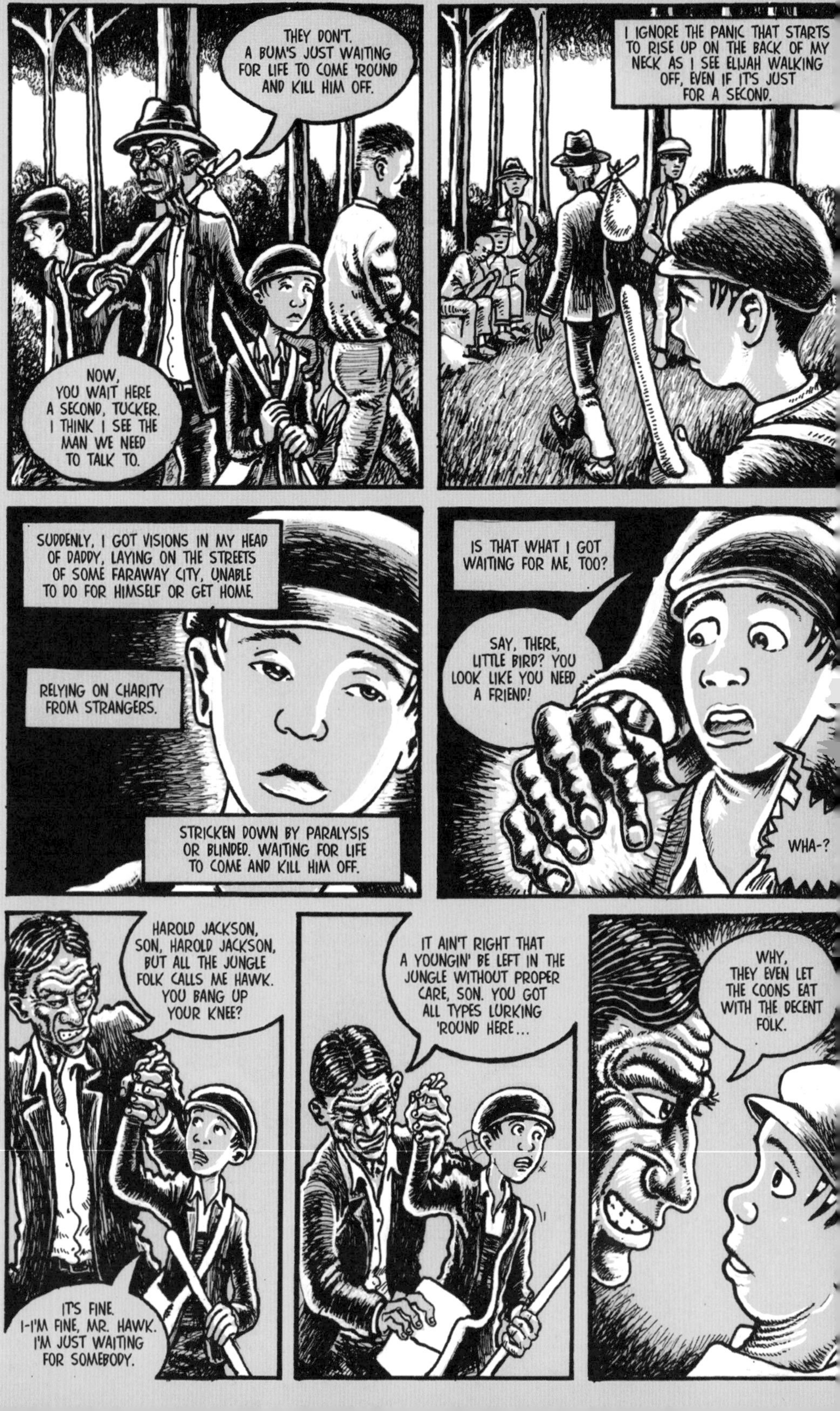
THEY DON'T. A BUM'S JUST WAITING FOR LIFE TO COME 'ROUND AND KILL HIM OFF.
NOW, YOU WAIT HERE A SECOND, TUCKER. I THINK I SEE THE MAN WE NEED TO TALK TO.
I IGNORE THE PANIC THAT STARTS TO RISE UP ON THE BACK OF MY NECK AS I SEE ELIJAH WALKING OFF, EVEN IF IT'S JUST FOR A SECOND.
SUDDENLY, I GOT VISIONS IN MY HEAD OF DADDY, LAYING ON THE STREETS OF SOME FARAWAY CITY, UNABLE TO DO FOR HIMSELF OR GET HOME.
RELYING ON CHARITY FROM STRANGERS.
STRICKEN DOWN BY PARALYSIS OR BLINDED. WAITING FOR LIFE TO COME AND KILL HIM OFF.
IS THAT WHAT I GOT WAITING FOR ME, TOO?
SAY, THERE, LITTLE BIRD? YOU LOOK LIKE YOU NEED A FRIEND!
WHA-?
HAROLD JACKSON, SON, HAROLD JACKSON, BUT ALL THE JUNGLE FOLK CALLS ME HAWK. YOU BANG UP YOUR KNEE?
IT'S FINE. I-I'M FINE, MR. HAWK. I'M JUST WAITING FOR SOMEBODY.
IT AIN'T RIGHT THAT A YOUNGIN' BE LEFT IN THE JUNGLE WITHOUT PROPER CARE, SON. YOU GOT ALL TYPES LURKING 'ROUND HERE...
WHY, THEY EVEN LET THE COONS EAT WITH THE DECENT FOLK.

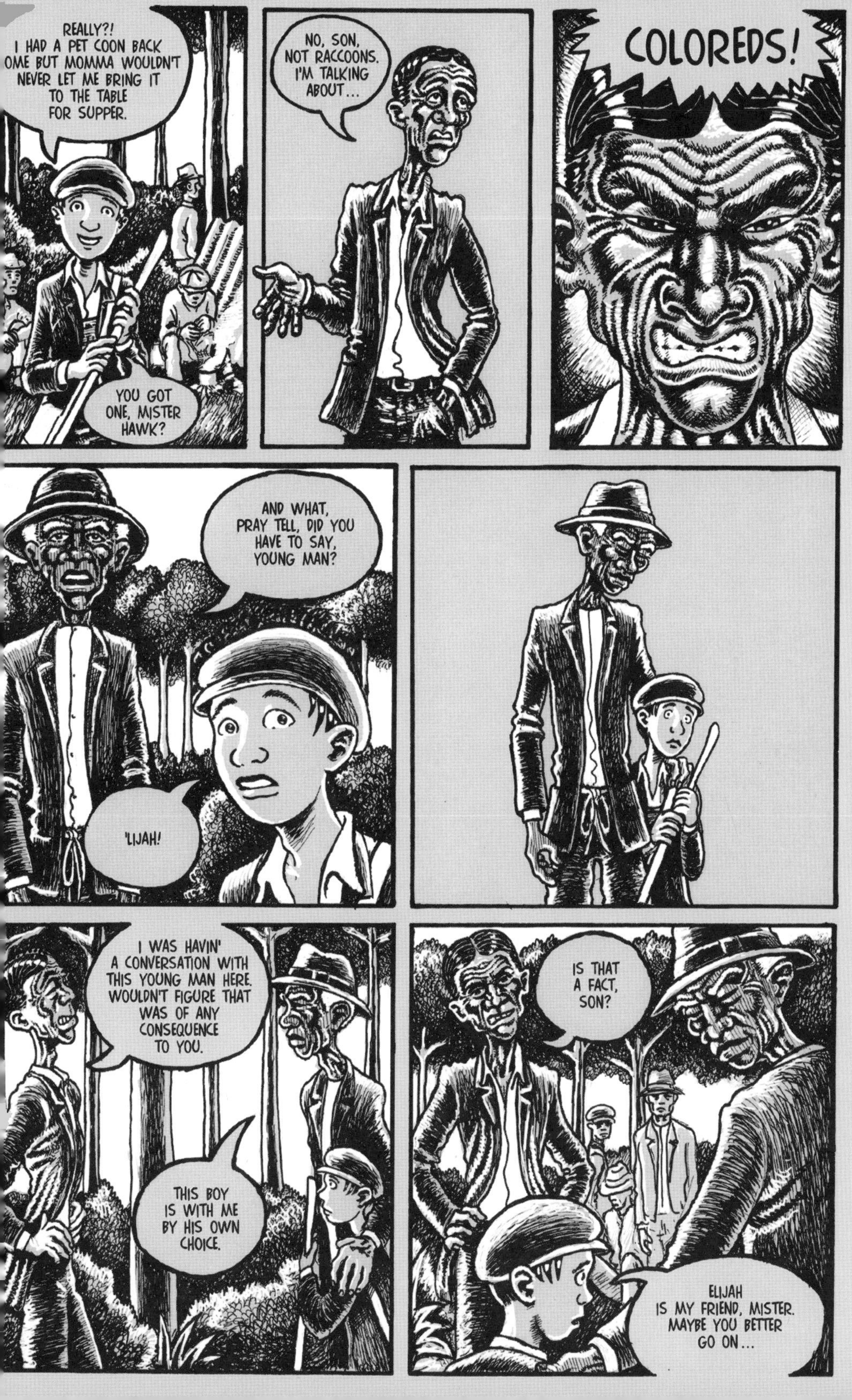
REALLY?! I HAD A PET COON BACK OME BUT MOMMA WOULDN'T NEVER LET ME BRING IT TO THE TABLE FOR SUPPER.
YOU GOT ONE, MISTER HAWK?
NO, SON, NOT RACCOONS. I'M TALKING ABOUT...
COLOREDS!
AND WHAT, PRAY TELL, DID YOU HAVE TO SAY, YOUNG MAN?
'LIJAH!
I WAS HAVIN' A CONVERSATION WITH THIS YOUNG MAN HERE. WOULDN'T FIGURE THAT WAS OF ANY CONSEQUENCE TO YOU.
THIS BOY IS WITH ME BY HIS OWN CHOICE.
IS THAT A FACT, SON?
ELIJAH IS MY FRIEND, MISTER. MAYBE YOU BETTER GO ON...

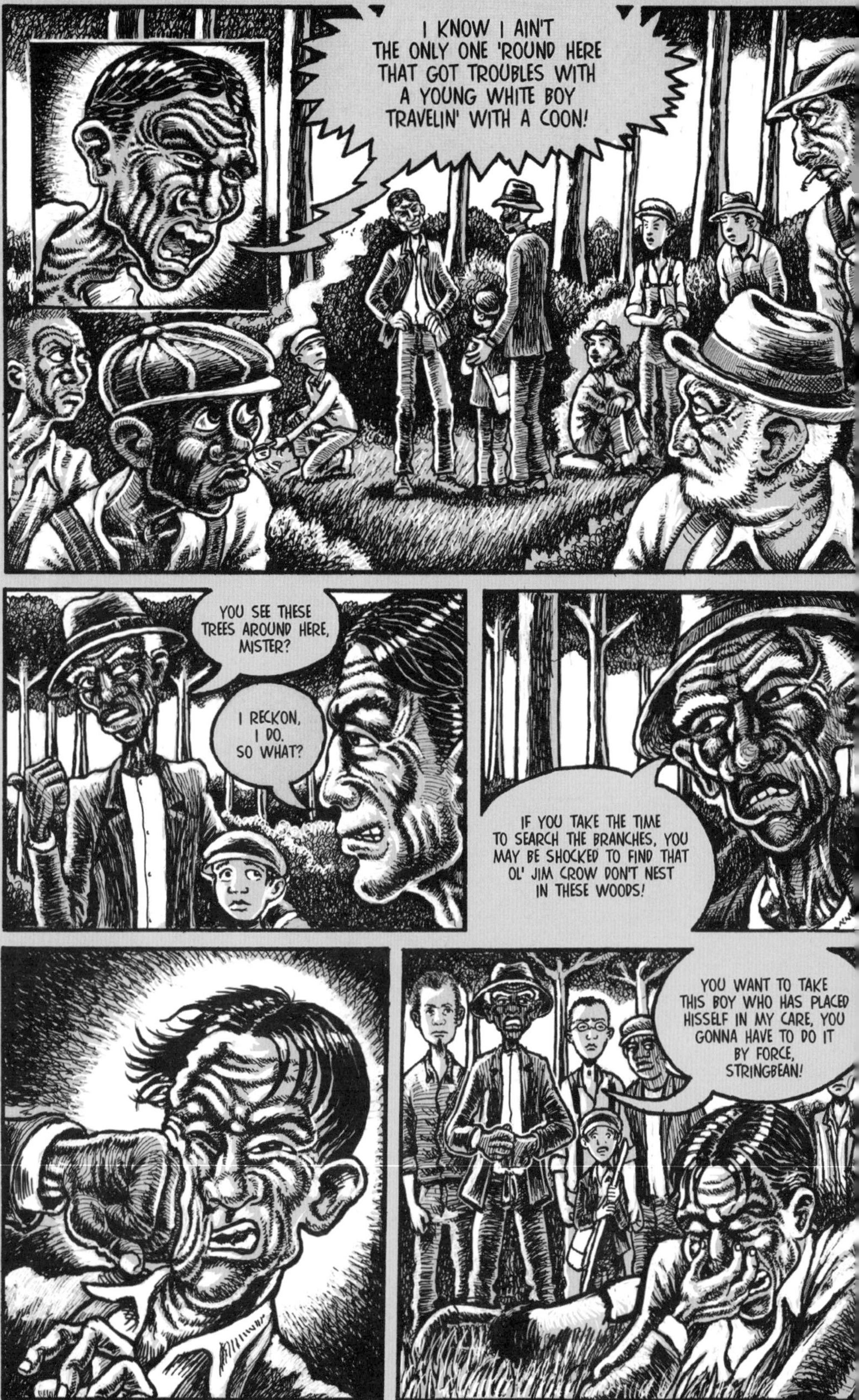
I KNOW I AIN'T THE ONLY ONE 'ROUND HERE THAT GOT TROUBLES WITH A YOUNG WHITE BOY TRAVELIN' WITH A COON!
YOU SEE THESE TREES AROUND HERE, MISTER?
I RECKON, I DO. SO WHAT?
IF YOU TAKE THE TIME TO SEARCH THE BRANCHES, YOU MAY BE SHOCKED TO FIND THAT OL' JIM CROW DON'T NEST IN THESE WOODS!
YOU WANT TO TAKE THIS BOY WHO HAS PLACED HISSELF IN MY CARE, YOU GONNA HAVE TO DO IT BY FORCE, STRINGBEAN!

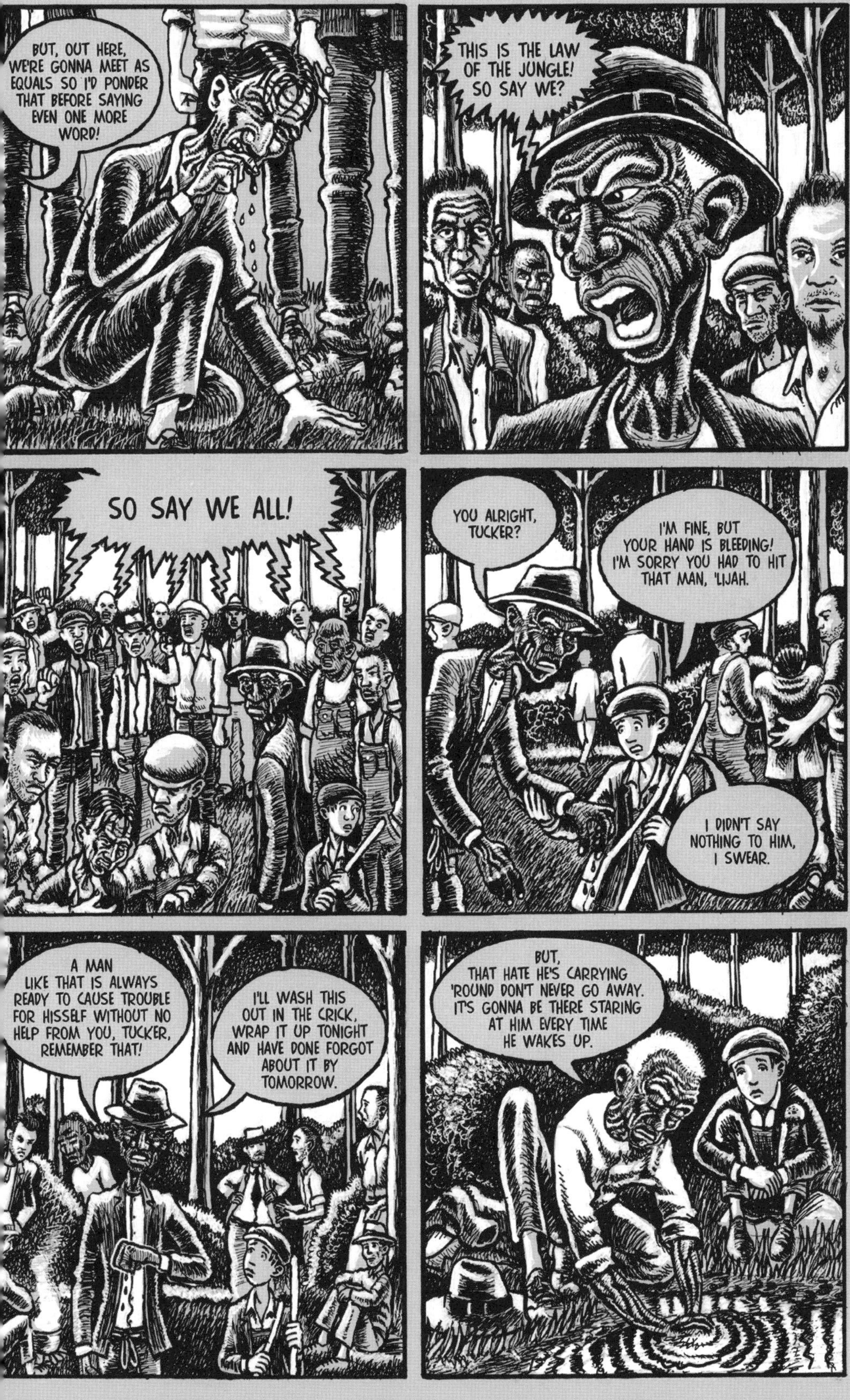
BUT, OUT HERE, WE'RE GONNA MEET AS EQUALS SO I'D PONDER THAT BEFORE SAYING EVEN ONE MORE WORD!
THIS IS THE LAW OF THE JUNGLE! SO SAY WE?
SO SAY WE ALL!
YOU ALRIGHT, TUCKER?
I'M FINE, BUT YOUR HAND IS BLEEDING! I'M SORRY YOU HAD TO HIT THAT MAN, 'LIJAH.
I DIDN'T SAY NOTHING TO HIM, I SWEAR.
A MAN LIKE THAT IS ALWAYS READY TO CAUSE TROUBLE FOR HISSELF WITHOUT NO HELP FROM YOU, TUCKER, REMEMBER THAT!
I'LL WASH THIS OUT IN THE CRICK, WRAP IT UP TONIGHT AND HAVE DONE FORGOT ABOUT IT BY TOMORROW.
BUT, THAT HATE HE'S CARRYING 'ROUND DON'T NEVER GO AWAY. IT'S GONNA BE THERE STARING AT HIM EVERY TIME HE WAKES UP.

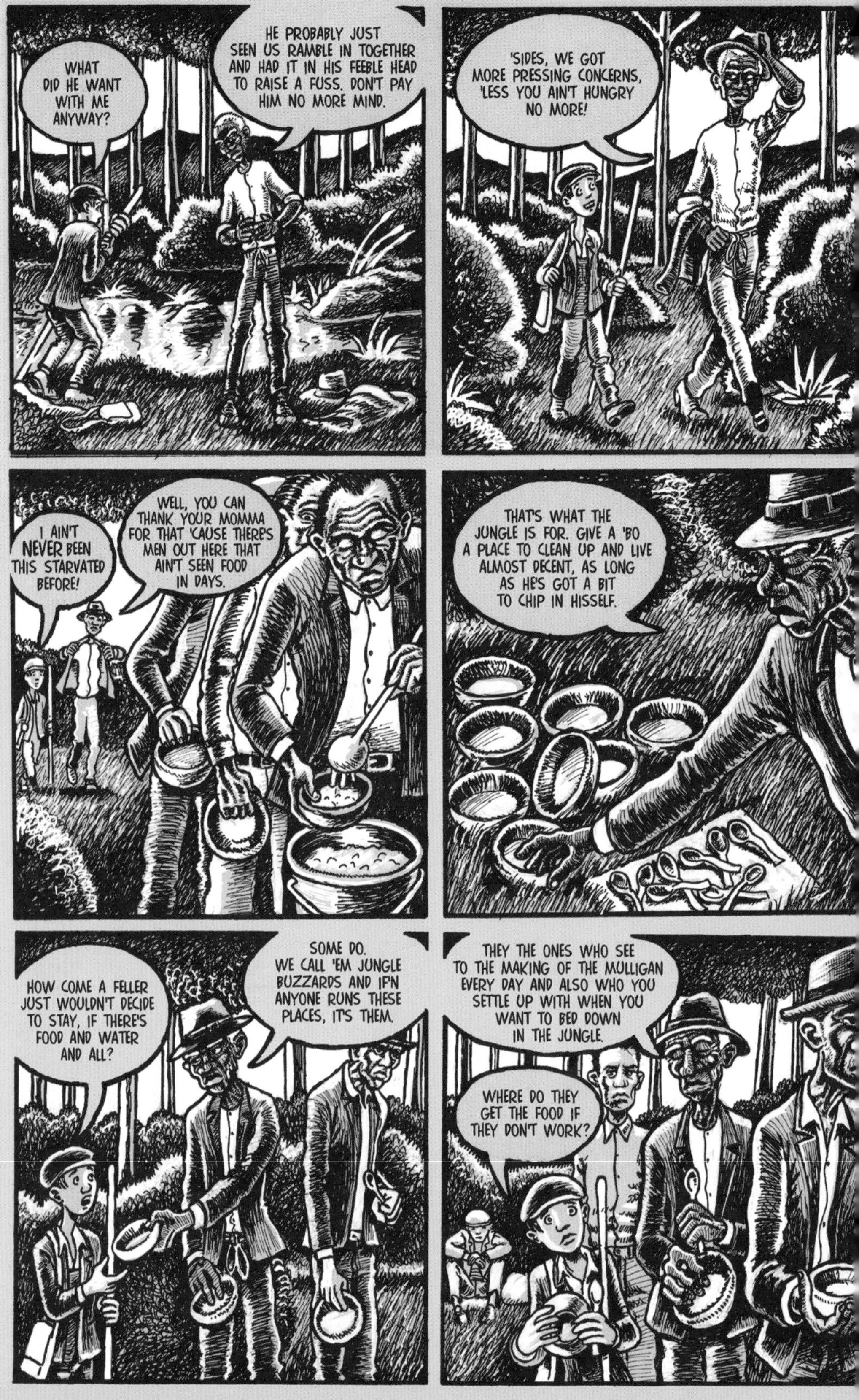
WHAT DID HE WANT WITH ME ANYWAY?
HE PROBABLY JUST SEEN US RAMBLE IN TOGETHER AND HAD IT IN HIS FEEBLE HEAD TO RAISE A FUSS. DON'T PAY HIM NO MORE MIND.
'SIDES, WE GOT MORE PRESSING CONCERNS, 'LESS YOU AIN'T HUNGRY NO MORE!
I AIN'T **NEVER** BEEN THIS STARVATED BEFORE!
WELL, YOU CAN THANK YOUR MOMMA FOR THAT 'CAUSE THERE'S MEN OUT HERE THAT AIN'T SEEN FOOD IN DAYS.
THAT'S WHAT THE JUNGLE IS FOR. GIVE A 'BO A PLACE TO CLEAN UP AND LIVE ALMOST DECENT, AS LONG AS HE'S GOT A BIT TO CHIP IN HISSELF.
HOW COME A FELLER JUST WOULDN'T DECIDE TO STAY, IF THERE'S FOOD AND WATER AND ALL?
SOME DO. WE CALL 'EM JUNGLE BUZZARDS AND IF'N ANYONE RUNS THESE PLACES, IT'S THEM.
THEY THE ONES WHO SEE TO THE MAKING OF THE MULLIGAN EVERY DAY AND ALSO WHO YOU SETTLE UP WITH WHEN YOU WANT TO BED DOWN IN THE JUNGLE.
WHERE DO THEY GET THE FOOD IF THEY DON'T WORK?

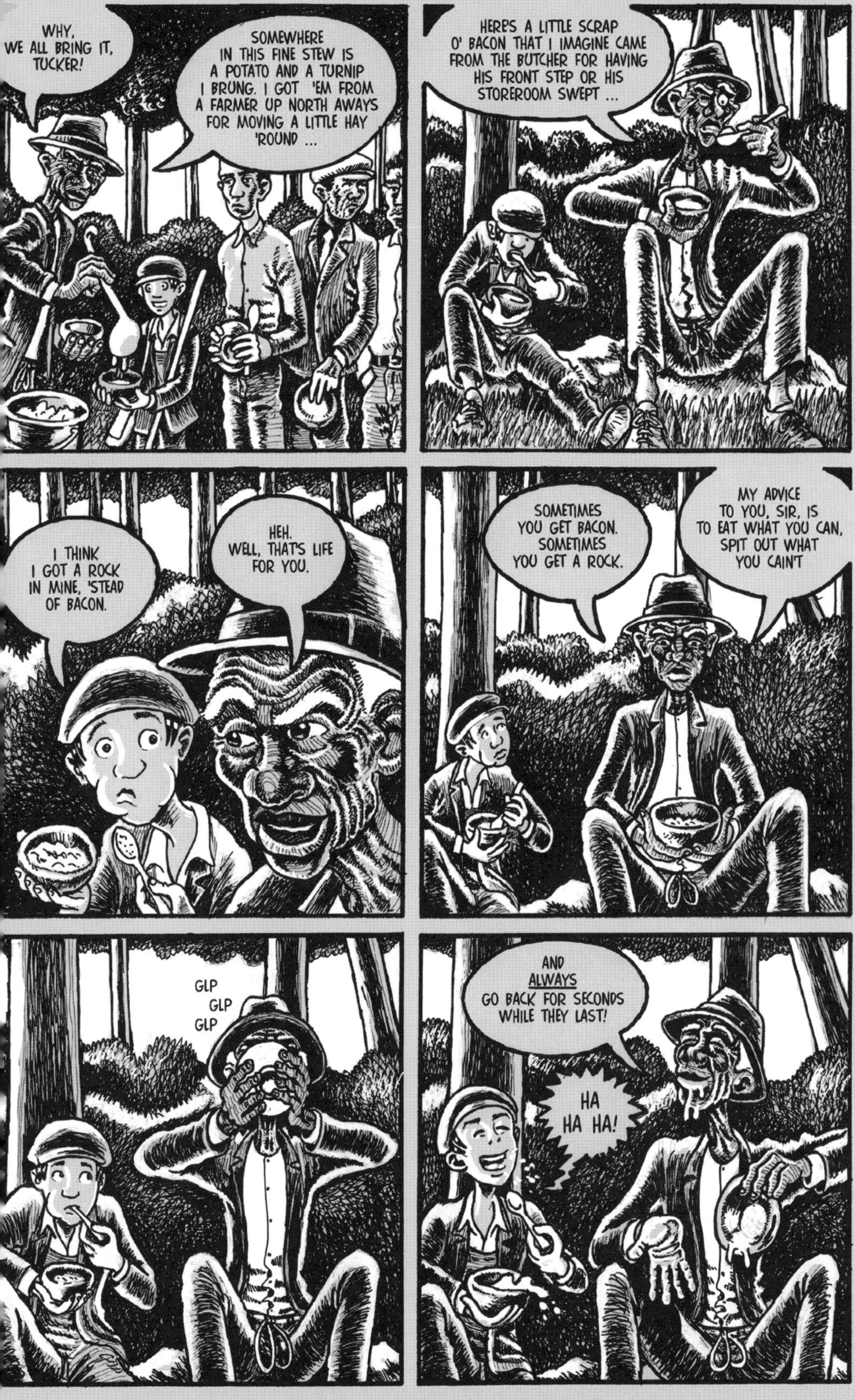
WHY, WE ALL BRING IT, TUCKER!
SOMEWHERE IN THIS FINE STEW IS A POTATO AND A TURNIP I BRUNG. I GOT 'EM FROM A FARMER UP NORTH AWAYS FOR MOVING A LITTLE HAY 'ROUND ...
HERE'S A LITTLE SCRAP O' BACON THAT I IMAGINE CAME FROM THE BUTCHER FOR HAVING HIS FRONT STEP OR HIS STOREROOM SWEPT ...
I THINK I GOT A ROCK IN MINE, 'STEAD OF BACON.
HEH. WELL, THAT'S LIFE FOR YOU.
SOMETIMES YOU GET BACON. SOMETIMES YOU GET A ROCK.
MY ADVICE TO YOU, SIR, IS TO EAT WHAT YOU CAN, SPIT OUT WHAT YOU CAIN'T
GLP GLP GLP
AND ALWAYS GO BACK FOR SECONDS WHILE THEY LAST!
HA HA HA!

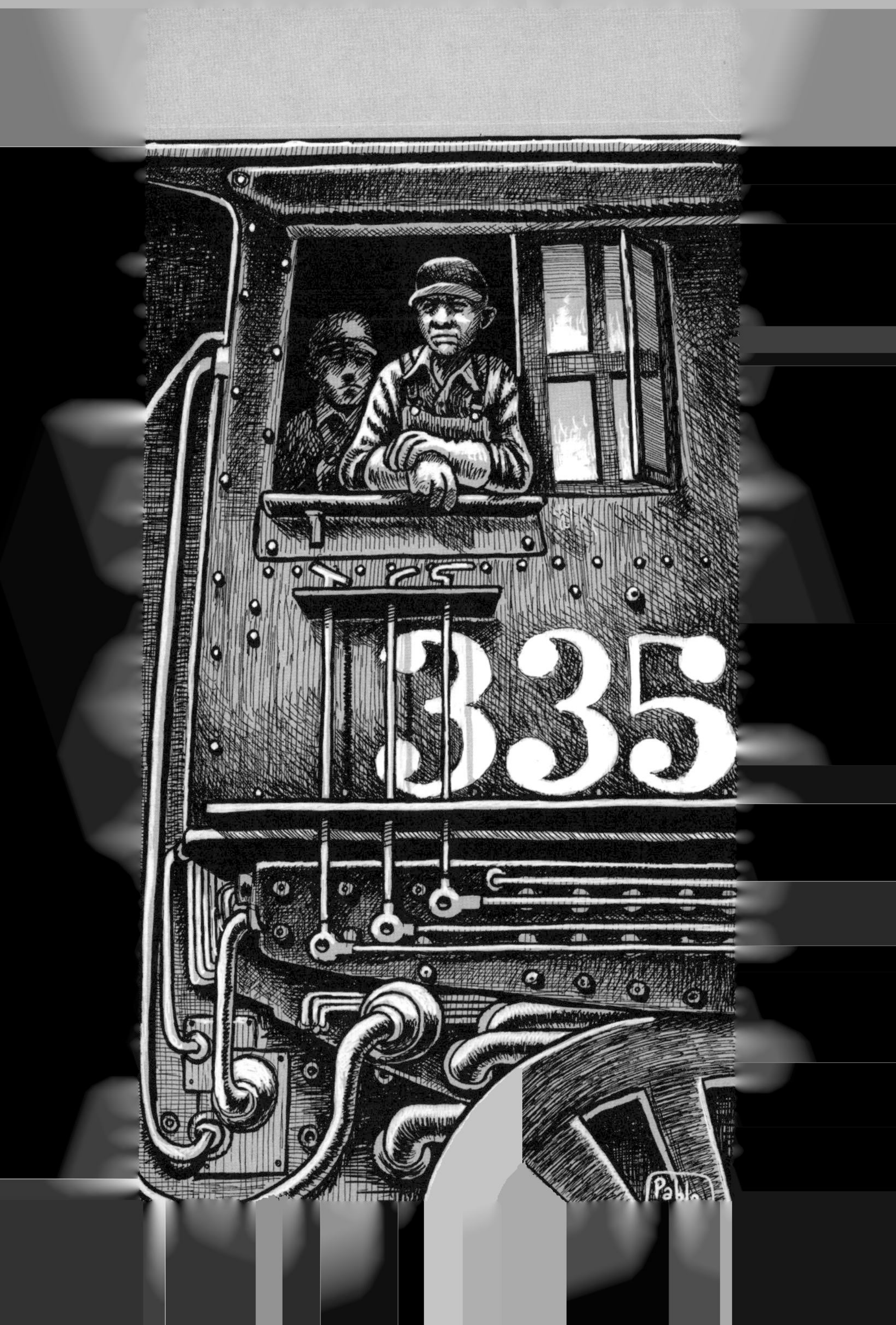
335
Pablo

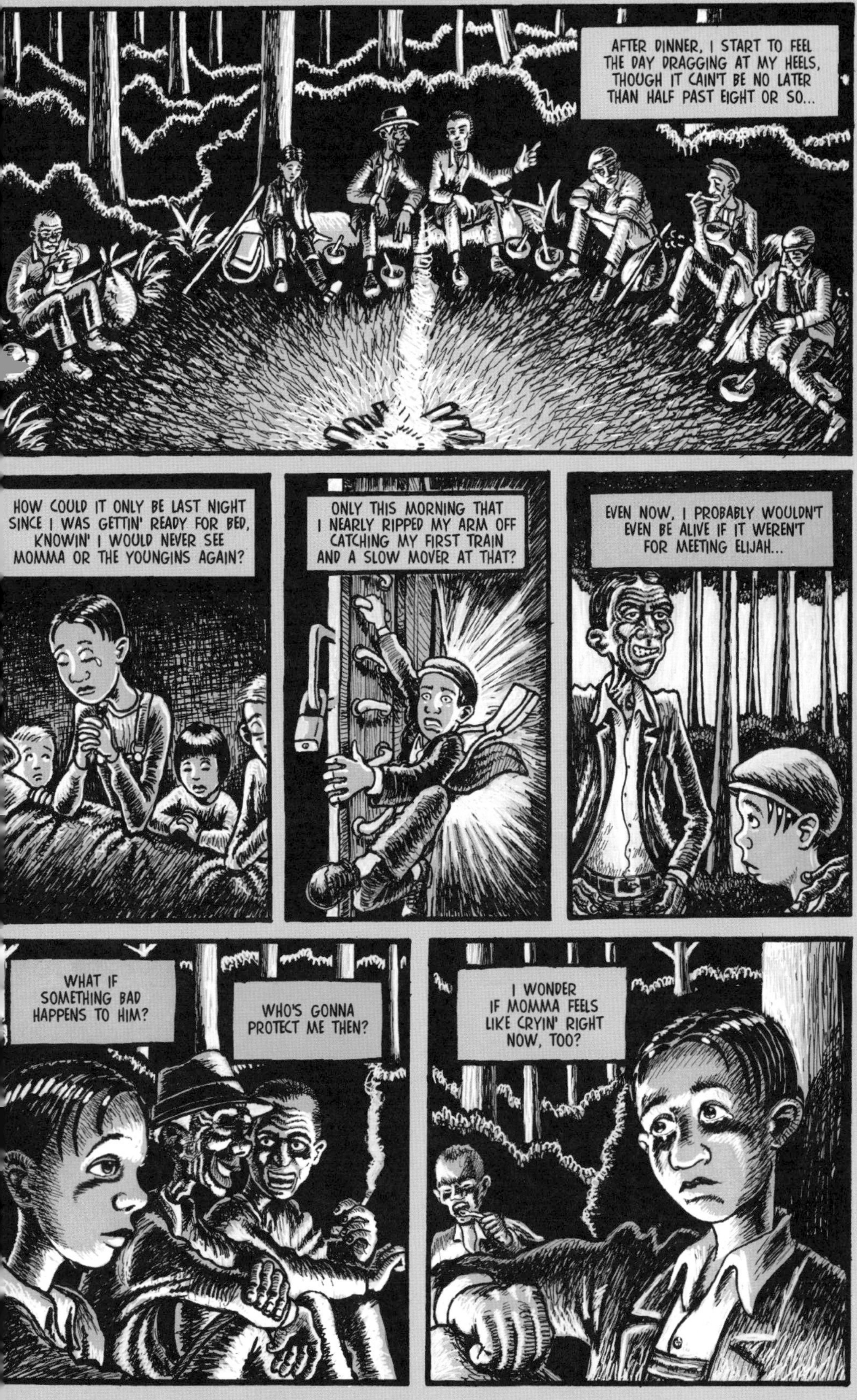
AFTER DINNER, I START TO FEEL THE DAY DRAGGING AT MY HEELS, THOUGH IT CAIN'T BE NO LATER THAN HALF PAST EIGHT OR SO...
HOW COULD IT ONLY BE LAST NIGHT SINCE I WAS GETTIN' READY FOR BED, KNOWIN' I WOULD NEVER SEE MOMMA OR THE YOUNGINS AGAIN?
ONLY THIS MORNING THAT I NEARLY RIPPED MY ARM OFF CATCHING MY FIRST TRAIN AND A SLOW MOVER AT THAT?
EVEN NOW, I PROBABLY WOULDN'T EVEN BE ALIVE IF IT WEREN'T FOR MEETING ELIJAH...
WHAT IF SOMETHING BAD HAPPENS TO HIM?
WHO'S GONNA PROTECT ME THEN?
I WONDER IF MOMMA FEELS LIKE CRYIN' RIGHT NOW, TOO?

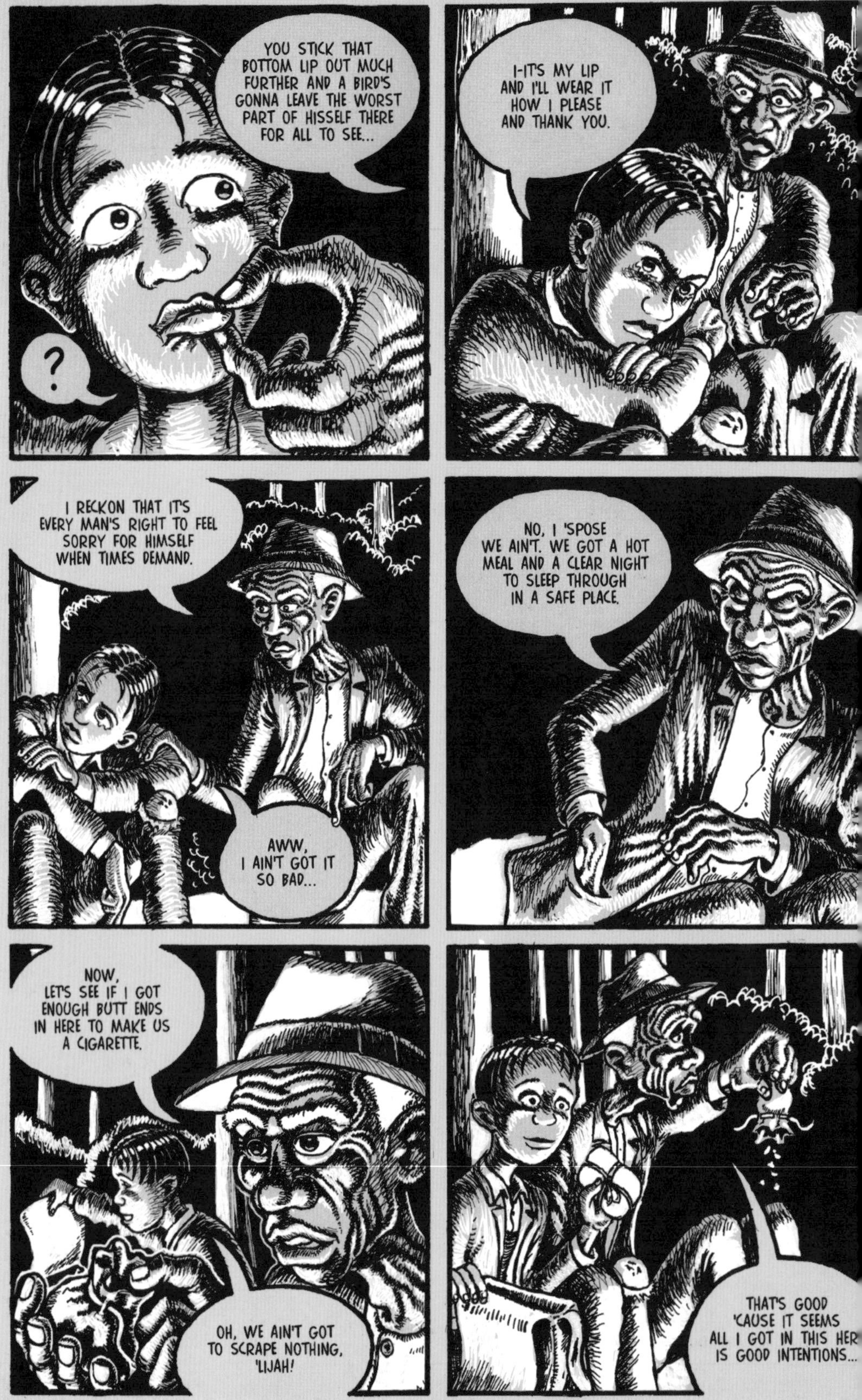
YOU STICK THAT BOTTOM LIP OUT MUCH FURTHER AND A BIRD'S GONNA LEAVE THE WORST PART OF HISSELF THERE FOR ALL TO SEE...
?
I-IT'S MY LIP AND I'LL WEAR IT HOW I PLEASE AND THANK YOU.
I RECKON THAT IT'S EVERY MAN'S RIGHT TO FEEL SORRY FOR HIMSELF WHEN TIMES DEMAND.
AWW, I AIN'T GOT IT SO BAD...
NO, I 'SPOSE WE AIN'T. WE GOT A HOT MEAL AND A CLEAR NIGHT TO SLEEP THROUGH IN A SAFE PLACE.
NOW, LET'S SEE IF I GOT ENOUGH BUTT ENDS IN HERE TO MAKE US A CIGARETTE.
OH, WE AIN'T GOT TO SCRAPE NOTHING, 'LIJAH!
THAT'S GOOD 'CAUSE IT SEEMS ALL I GOT IN THIS HER IS GOOD INTENTIONS...

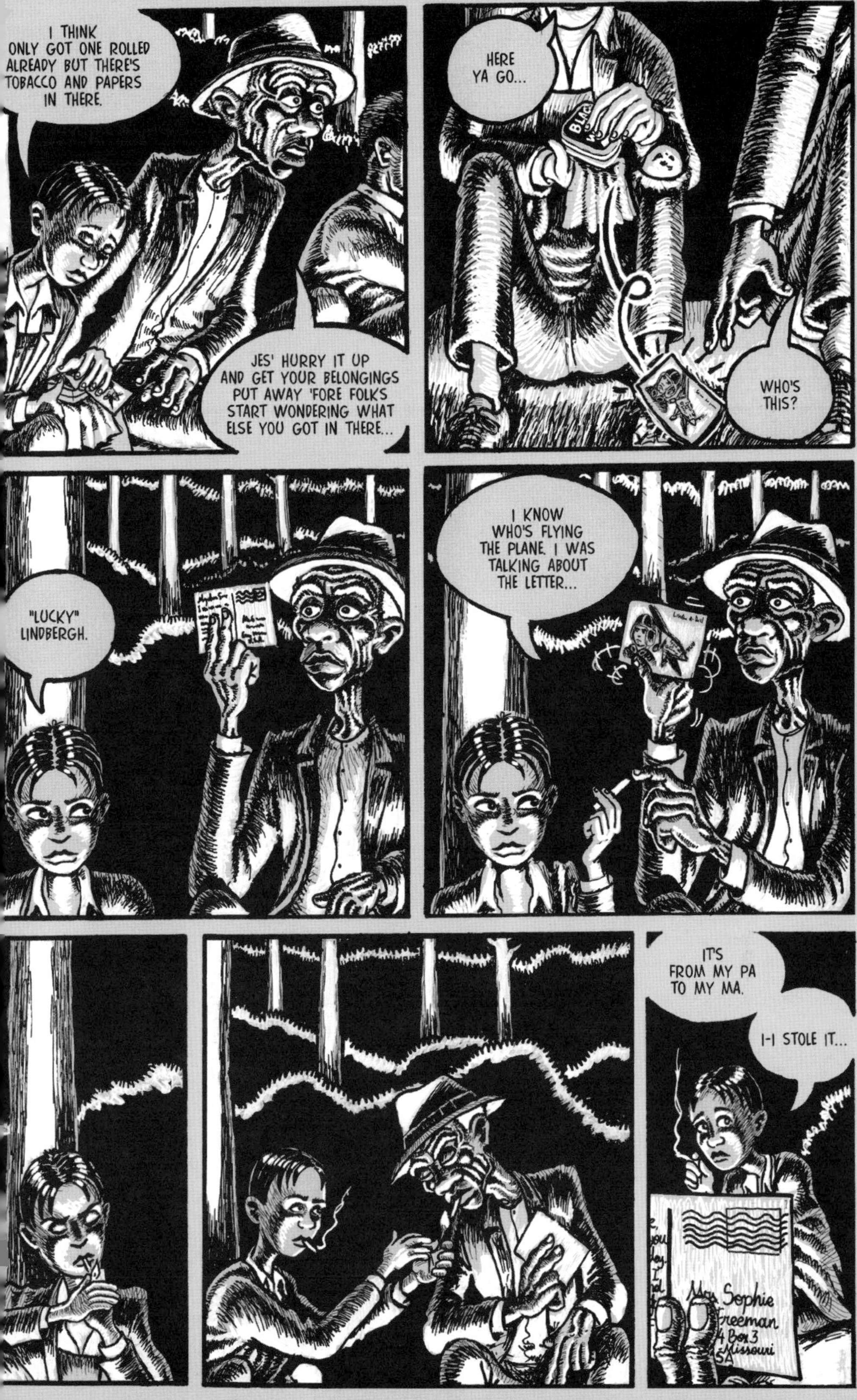
I THINK ONLY GOT ONE ROLLED ALREADY BUT THERE'S TOBACCO AND PAPERS IN THERE.
JES' HURRY IT UP AND GET YOUR BELONGINGS PUT AWAY 'FORE FOLKS START WONDERING WHAT ELSE YOU GOT IN THERE...
HERE YA GO...
WHO'S THIS?
"LUCKY" LINDBERGH.
I KNOW WHO'S FLYING THE PLANE. I WAS TALKING ABOUT THE LETTER...
IT'S FROM MY PA TO MY MA.
I-I STOLE IT...

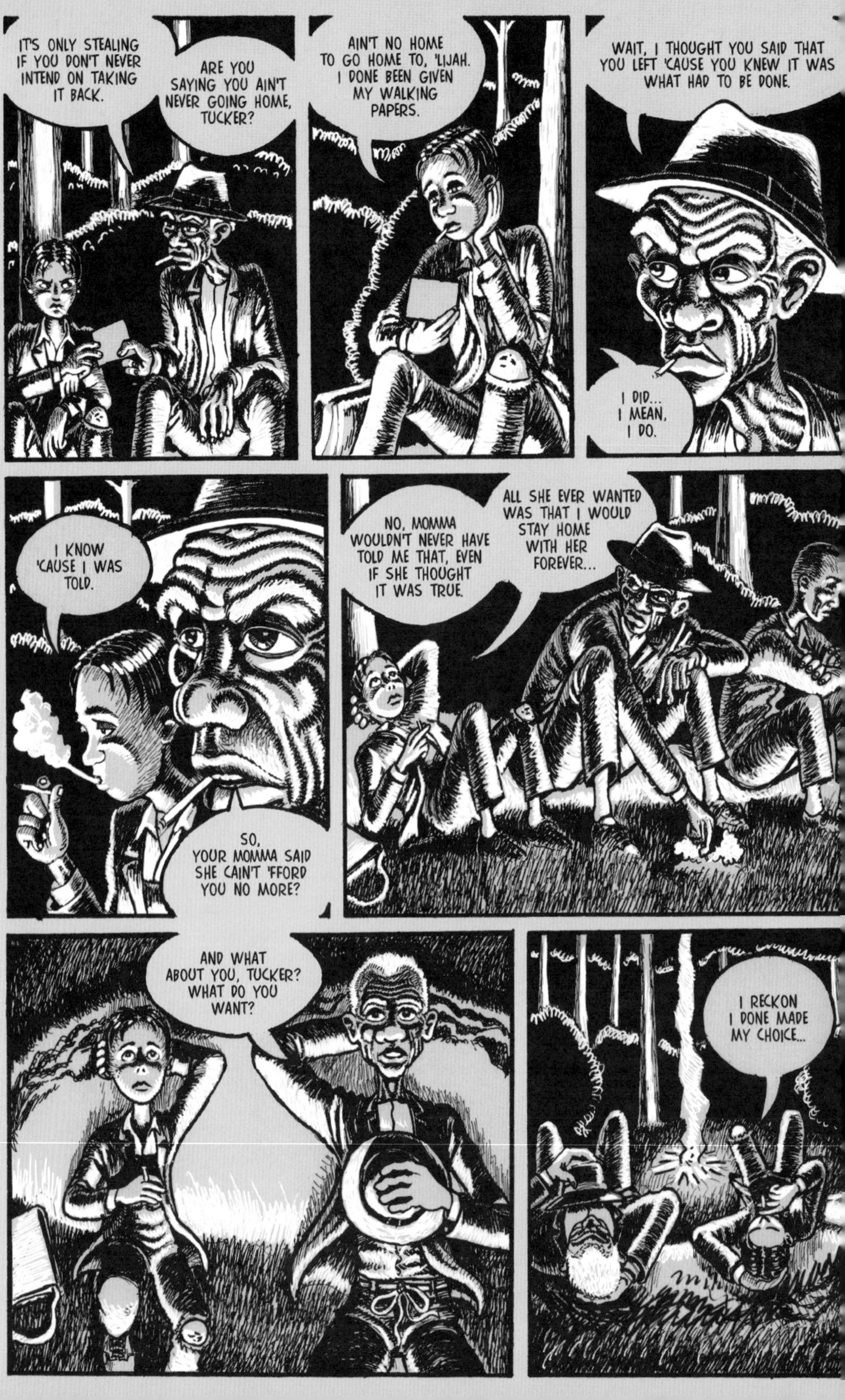
IT'S ONLY STEALING IF YOU DON'T NEVER INTEND ON TAKING IT BACK.
ARE YOU SAYING YOU AIN'T NEVER GOING HOME, TUCKER?
AIN'T NO HOME TO GO HOME TO, 'LIJAH. I DONE BEEN GIVEN MY WALKING PAPERS.
WAIT, I THOUGHT YOU SAID THAT YOU LEFT 'CAUSE YOU KNEW IT WAS WHAT HAD TO BE DONE.
I DID... I MEAN, I DO.
I KNOW 'CAUSE I WAS TOLD.
SO, YOUR MOMMA SAID SHE CAIN'T 'FFORD YOU NO MORE?
NO, MOMMA WOULDN'T NEVER HAVE TOLD ME THAT, EVEN IF SHE THOUGHT IT WAS TRUE.
ALL SHE EVER WANTED WAS THAT I WOULD STAY HOME WITH HER FOREVER...
AND WHAT ABOUT YOU, TUCKER? WHAT DO YOU WANT?
I RECKON I DONE MADE MY CHOICE...

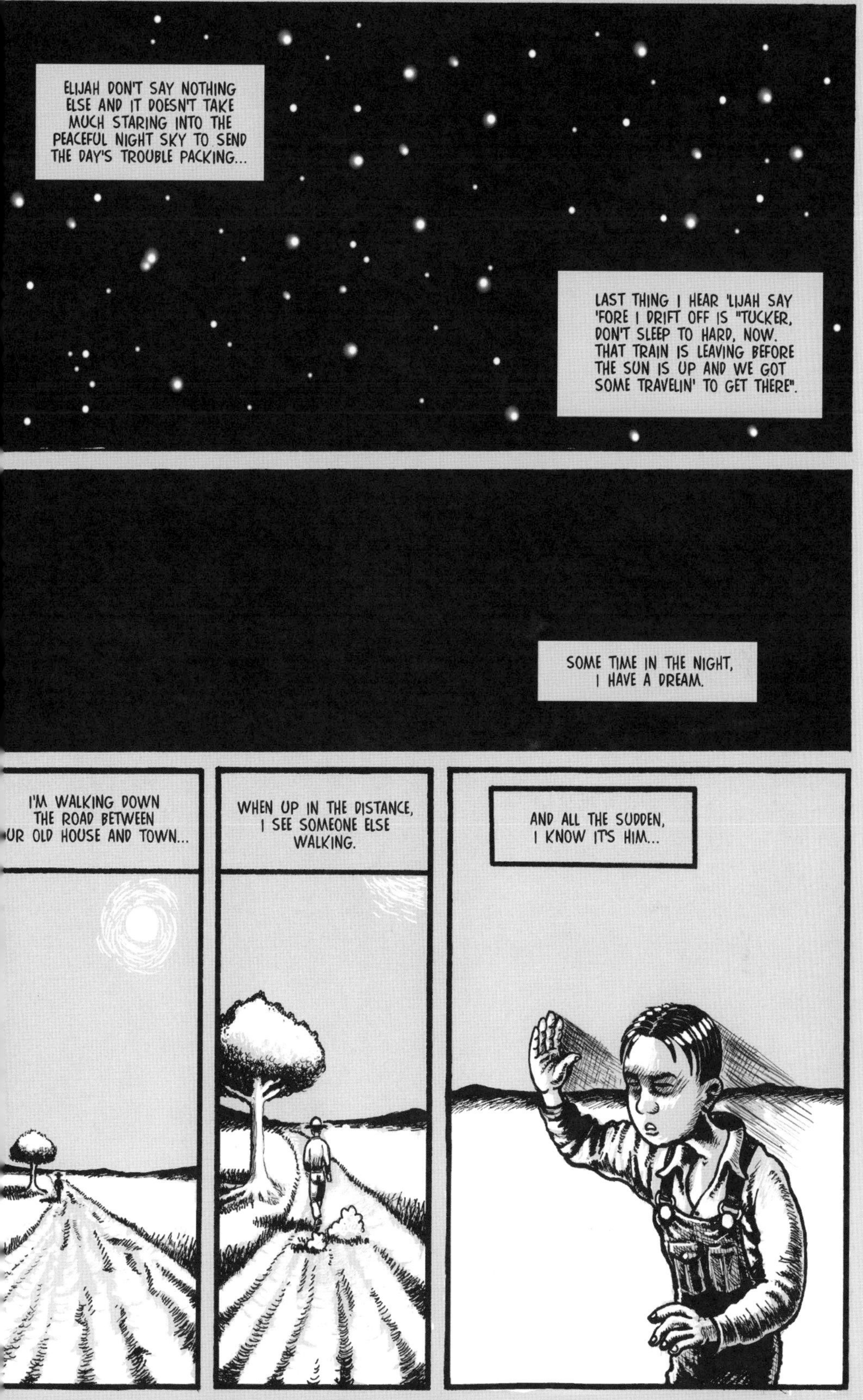
ELIJAH DON'T SAY NOTHING ELSE AND IT DOESN'T TAKE MUCH STARING INTO THE PEACEFUL NIGHT SKY TO SEND THE DAY'S TROUBLE PACKING...
LAST THING I HEAR 'LIJAH SAY 'FORE I DRIFT OFF IS "TUCKER, DON'T SLEEP TO HARD, NOW. THAT TRAIN IS LEAVING BEFORE THE SUN IS UP AND WE GOT SOME TRAVELIN' TO GET THERE".
SOME TIME IN THE NIGHT, I HAVE A DREAM.
I'M WALKING DOWN THE ROAD BETWEEN UR OLD HOUSE AND TOWN...
WHEN UP IN THE DISTANCE, I SEE SOMEONE ELSE WALKING.
AND ALL THE SUDDEN, I KNOW IT'S HIM...

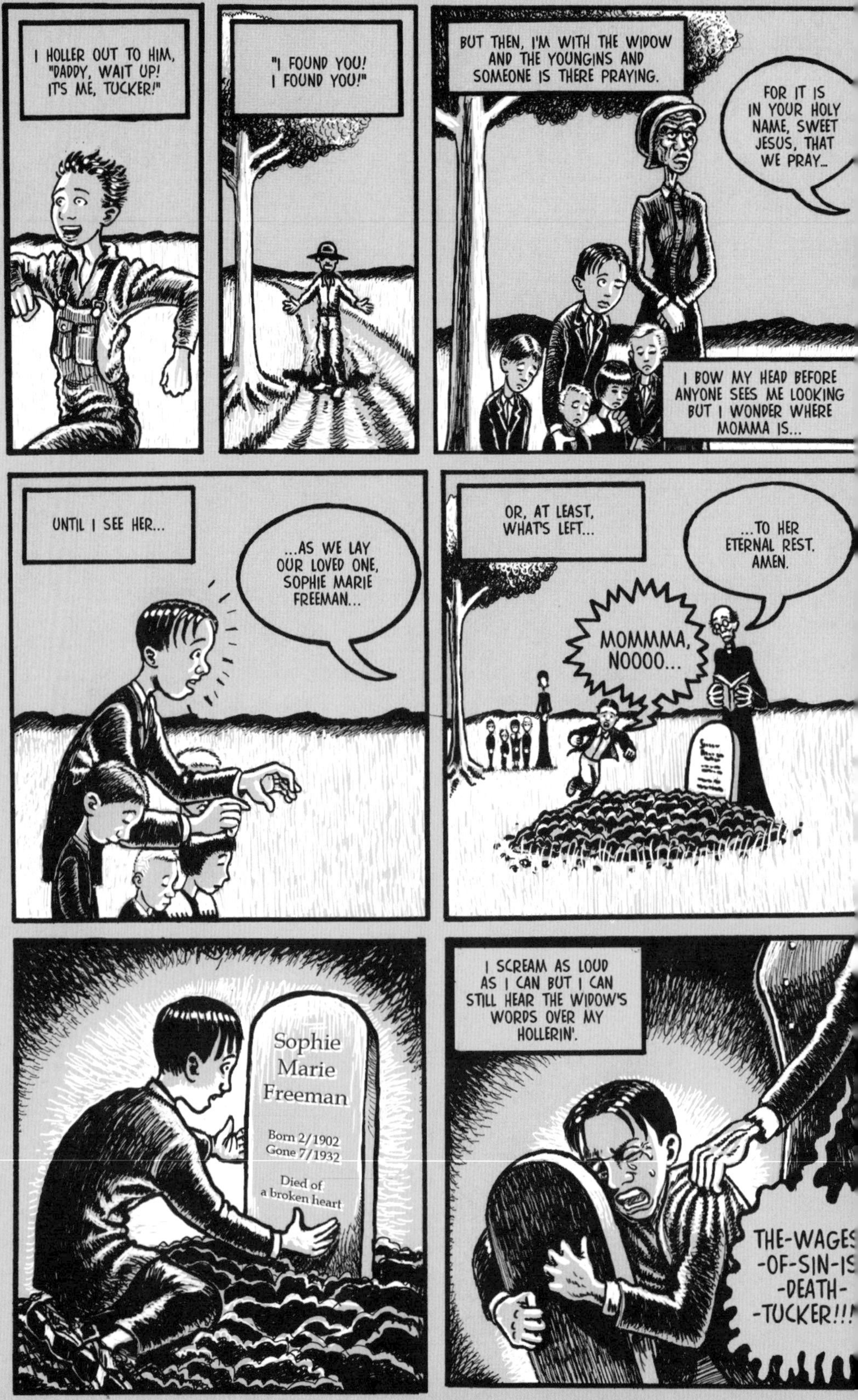
I HOLLER OUT TO HIM, "DADDY, WAIT UP! IT'S ME, TUCKER!"
"I FOUND YOU! I FOUND YOU!"
BUT THEN, I'M WITH THE WIDOW AND THE YOUNGINS AND SOMEONE IS THERE PRAYING.
FOR IT IS IN YOUR HOLY NAME, SWEET JESUS, THAT WE PRAY...
I BOW MY HEAD BEFORE ANYONE SEES ME LOOKING BUT I WONDER WHERE MOMMA IS...
UNTIL I SEE HER...
...AS WE LAY OUR LOVED ONE, SOPHIE MARIE FREEMAN...
OR, AT LEAST, WHAT'S LEFT...
...TO HER ETERNAL REST. AMEN.
MOMMMA, NOOOO...
Sophie Marie Freeman
Born 2/1902
Gone 7/1932
Died of a broken heart
I SCREAM AS LOUD AS I CAN BUT I CAN STILL HEAR THE WIDOW'S WORDS OVER MY HOLLERIN'.
THE-WAGES -OF-SIN-IS -DEATH- -TUCKER!!!

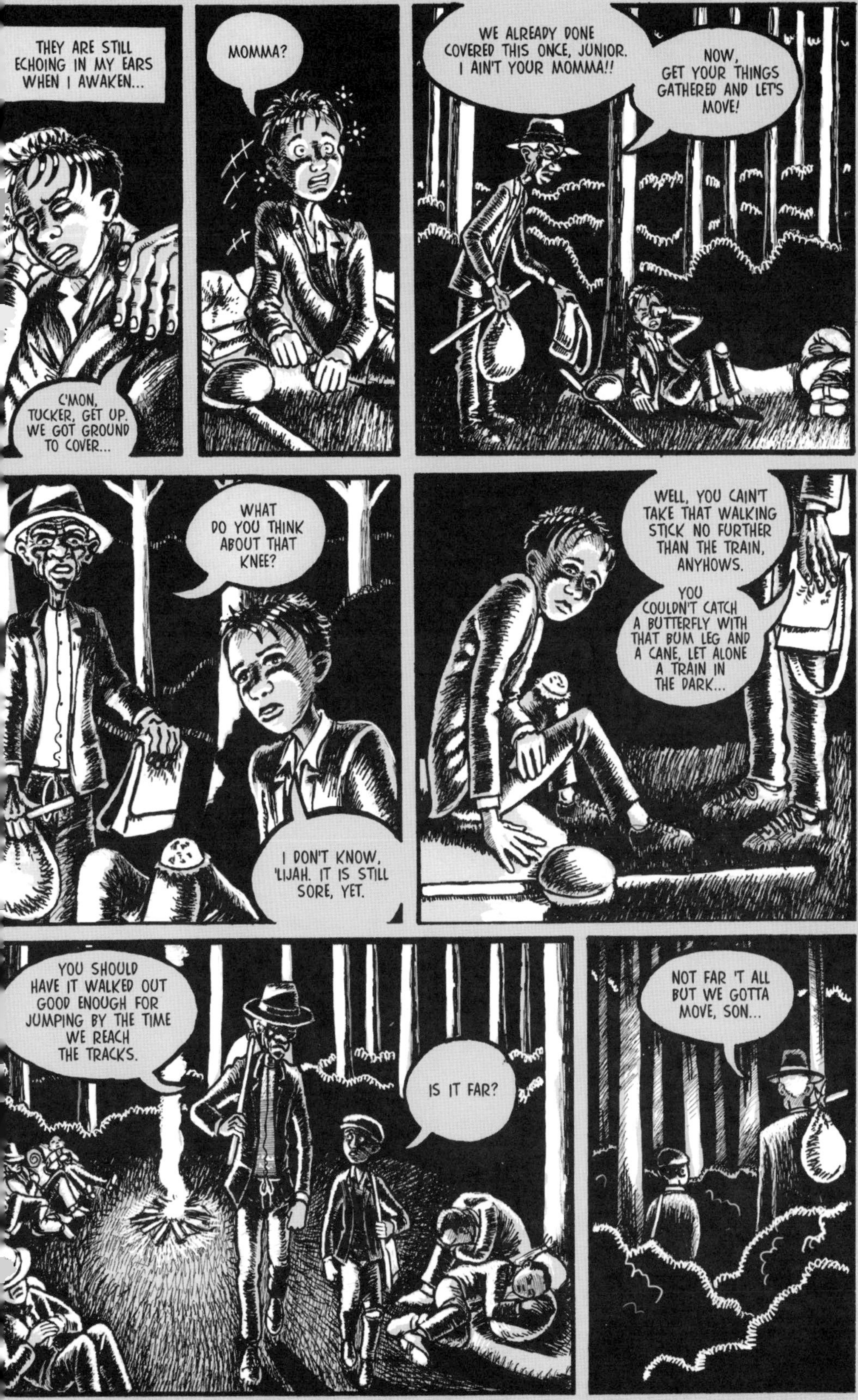
THEY ARE STILL ECHOING IN MY EARS WHEN I AWAKEN...
C'MON, TUCKER, GET UP. WE GOT GROUND TO COVER...
MOMMA?
WE ALREADY DONE COVERED THIS ONCE, JUNIOR. I AIN'T YOUR MOMMA!!
NOW, GET YOUR THINGS GATHERED AND LET'S MOVE!
WHAT DO YOU THINK ABOUT THAT KNEE?
I DON'T KNOW, 'LIJAH. IT IS STILL SORE, YET.
WELL, YOU CAIN'T TAKE THAT WALKING STICK NO FURTHER THAN THE TRAIN, ANYHOWS.
YOU COULDN'T CATCH A BUTTERFLY WITH THAT BUM LEG AND A CANE, LET ALONE A TRAIN IN THE DARK...
YOU SHOULD HAVE IT WALKED OUT GOOD ENOUGH FOR JUMPING BY THE TIME WE REACH THE TRACKS.
IS IT FAR?
NOT FAR 'T ALL BUT WE GOTTA MOVE, SON...

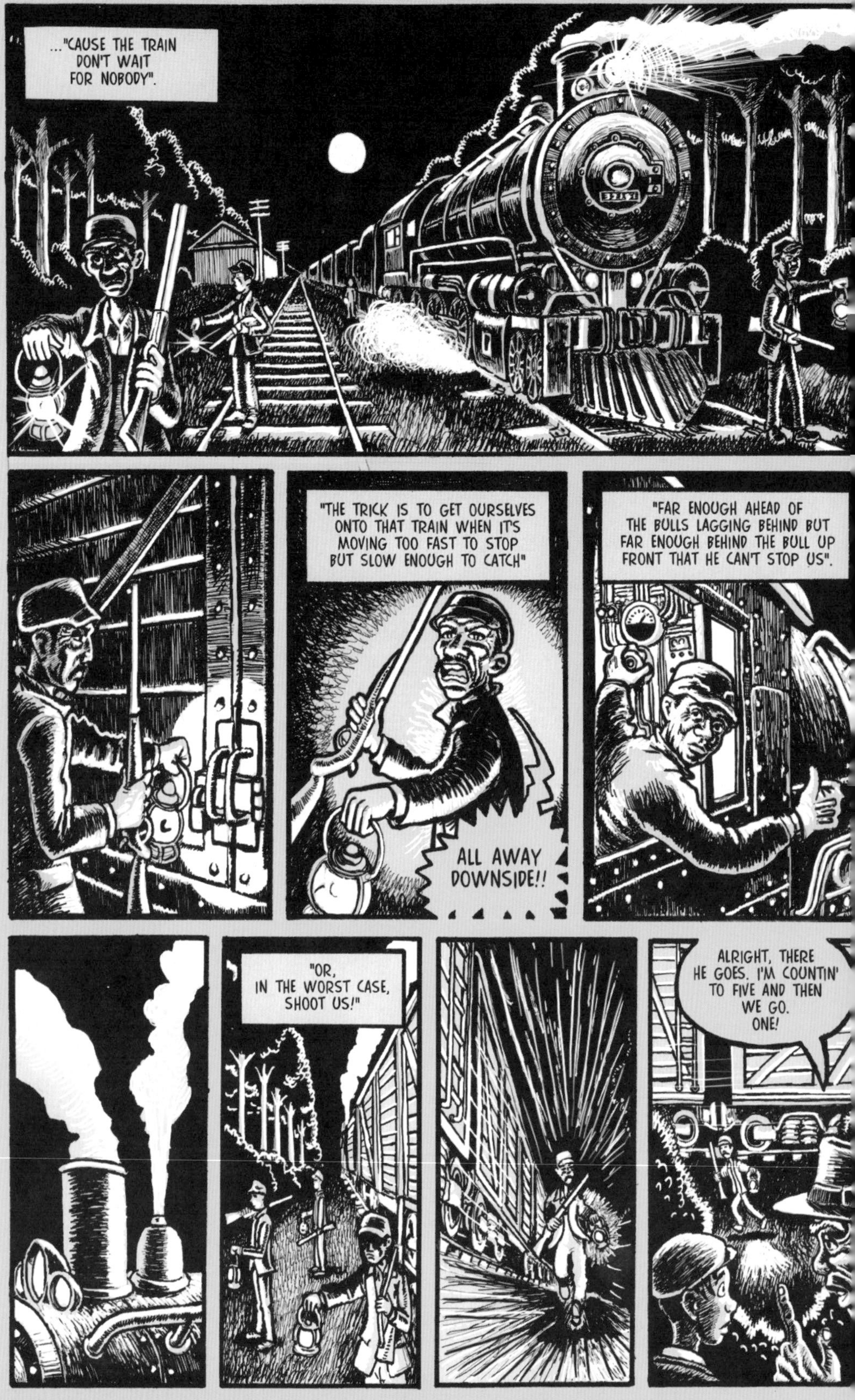
..."CAUSE THE TRAIN DON'T WAIT FOR NOBODY".
"THE TRICK IS TO GET OURSELVES ONTO THAT TRAIN WHEN IT'S MOVING TOO FAST TO STOP BUT SLOW ENOUGH TO CATCH"
ALL AWAY DOWNSIDE!!
"FAR ENOUGH AHEAD OF THE BULLS LAGGING BEHIND BUT FAR ENOUGH BEHIND THE BULL UP FRONT THAT HE CAN'T STOP US".
"OR, IN THE WORST CASE, SHOOT US!"
ALRIGHT, THERE HE GOES. I'M COUNTIN' TO FIVE AND THEN WE GO. ONE!

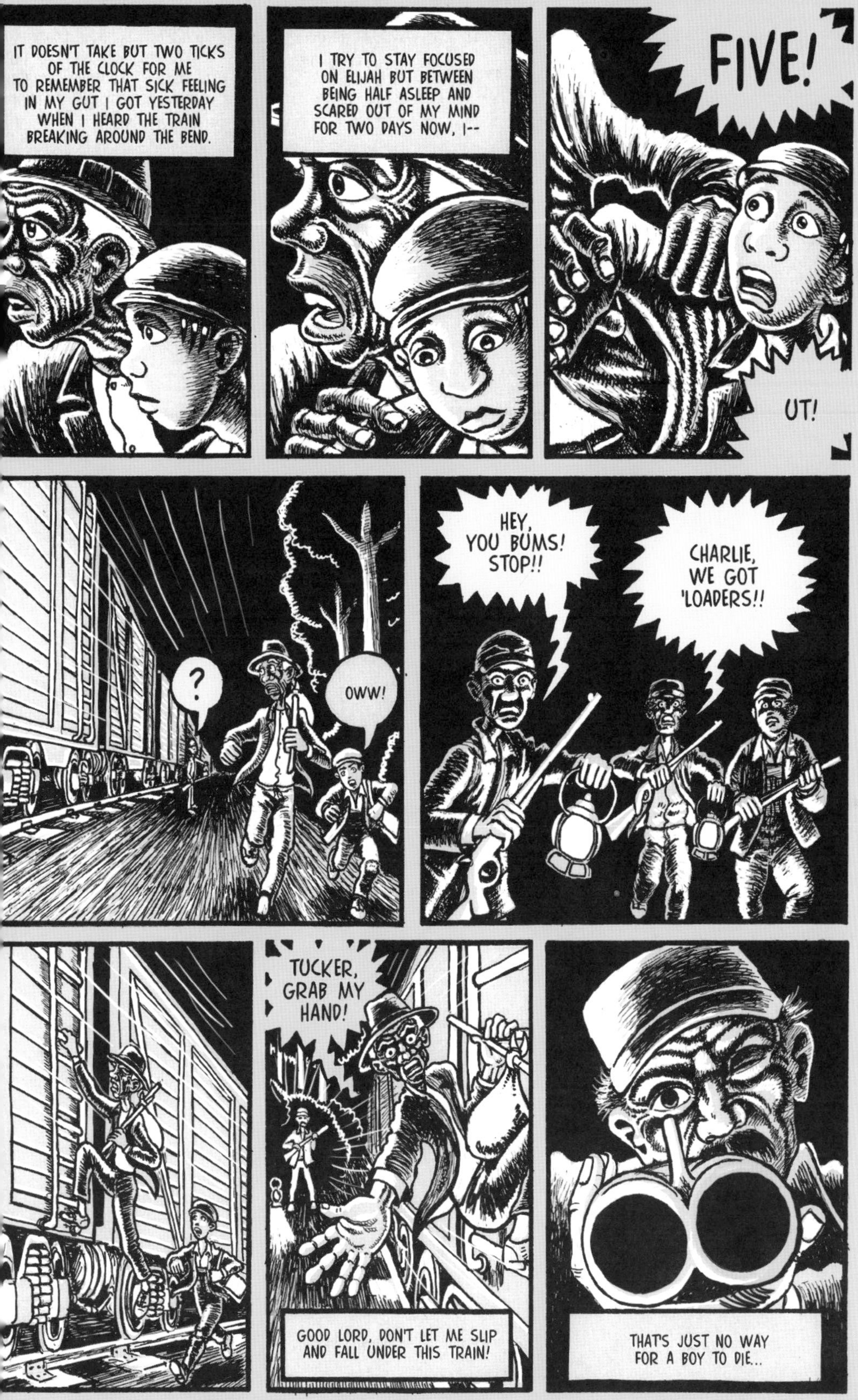
IT DOESN'T TAKE BUT TWO TICKS OF THE CLOCK FOR ME TO REMEMBER THAT SICK FEELING IN MY GUT I GOT YESTERDAY WHEN I HEARD THE TRAIN BREAKING AROUND THE BEND.
I TRY TO STAY FOCUSED ON ELIJAH BUT BETWEEN BEING HALF ASLEEP AND SCARED OUT OF MY MIND FOR TWO DAYS NOW, I--
FIVE!
UT!
?
OWW!
HEY, YOU BUMS! STOP!!
CHARLIE, WE GOT 'LOADERS!!
TUCKER, GRAB MY HAND!
GOOD LORD, DON'T LET ME SLIP AND FALL UNDER THIS TRAIN!
THAT'S JUST NO WAY FOR A BOY TO DIE...

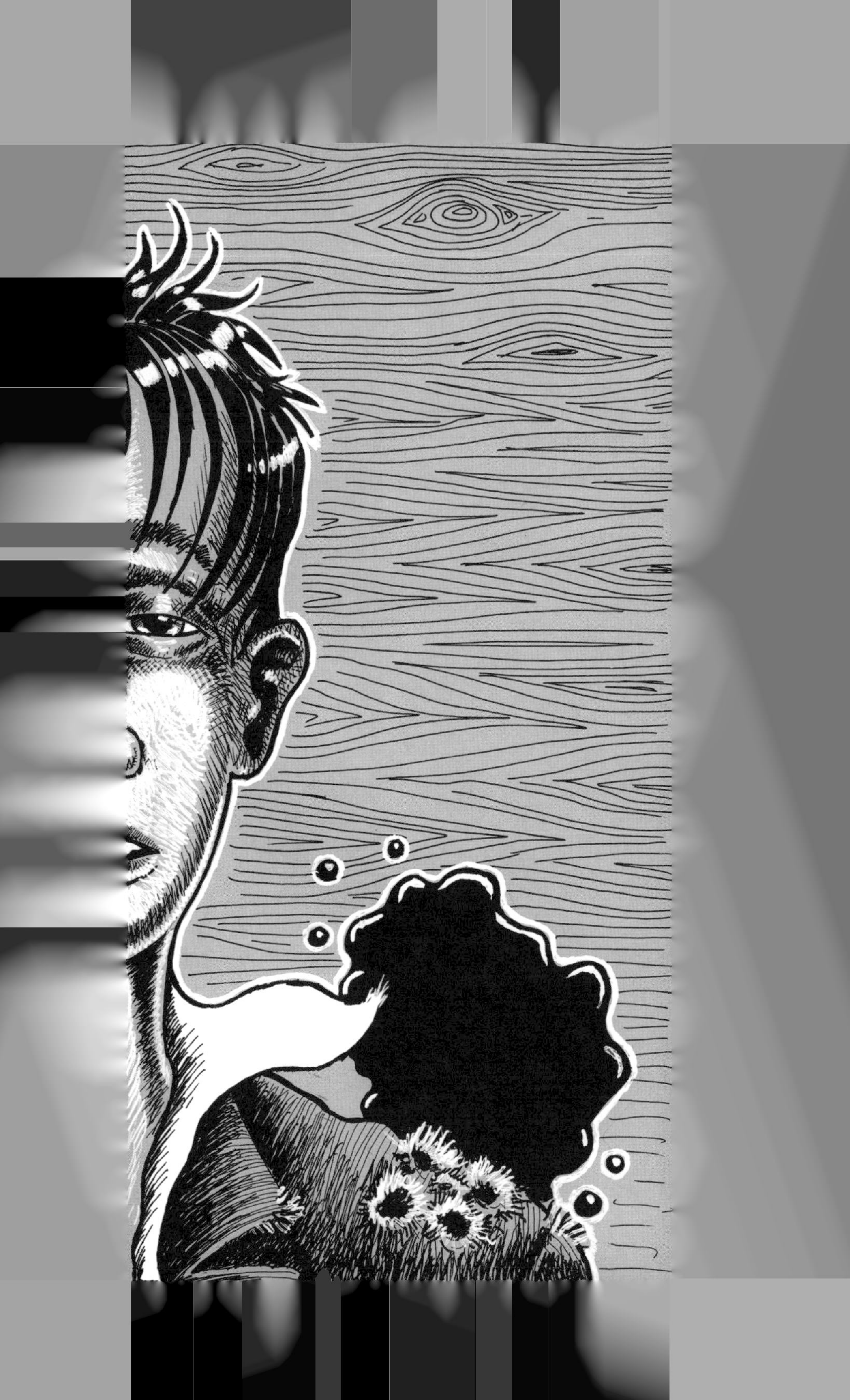

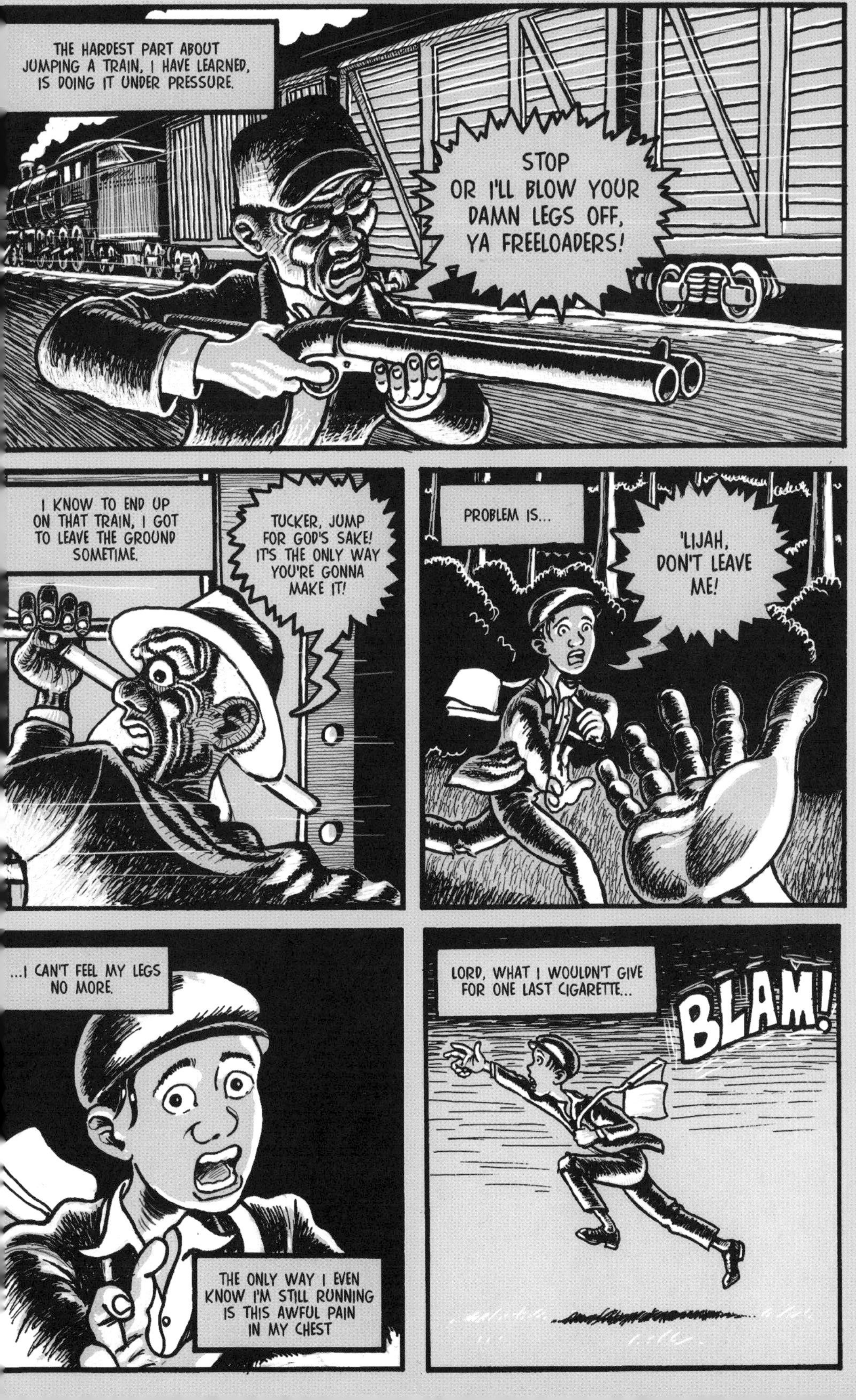
THE HARDEST PART ABOUT JUMPING A TRAIN, I HAVE LEARNED, IS DOING IT UNDER PRESSURE.
STOP OR I'LL BLOW YOUR DAMN LEGS OFF, YA FREELOADERS!
I KNOW TO END UP ON THAT TRAIN, I GOT TO LEAVE THE GROUND SOMETIME.
TUCKER, JUMP FOR GOD'S SAKE! IT'S THE ONLY WAY YOU'RE GONNA MAKE IT!
PROBLEM IS...
'LIJAH, DON'T LEAVE ME!
...I CAN'T FEEL MY LEGS NO MORE.
THE ONLY WAY I EVEN KNOW I'M STILL RUNNING IS THIS AWFUL PAIN IN MY CHEST
LORD, WHAT I WOULDN'T GIVE FOR ONE LAST CIGARETTE...
BLAM!

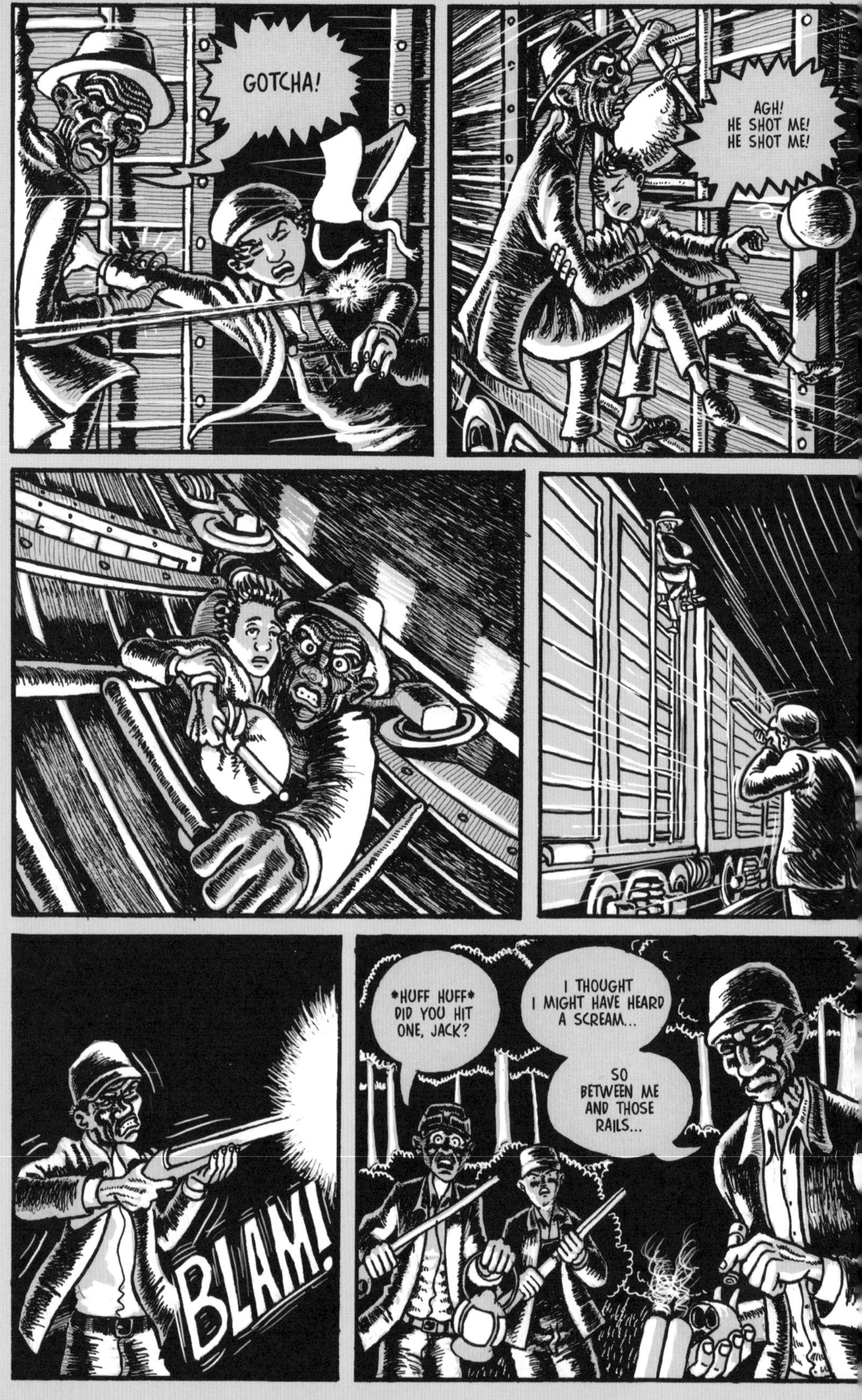
GOTCHA!
AGH! HE SHOT ME! HE SHOT ME!
BLAM!
HUFF HUFF DID YOU HIT ONE, JACK?
I THOUGHT I MIGHT HAVE HEARD A SCREAM...
SO BETWEEN ME AND THOSE RAILS...

"...I RECKON JUSTICE WAS SERVED HERE TODAY".

. . .

SWEET LORD A' MERCY, SON. DON'T MOVE 'TIL I SEEN WHAT KIND OF TROUBLE YOU'RE IN...

'LIJAH. IT BURNS...

WE'RE LUCKY WE'RE BOTH NOT DEAD UNDER THE WHEELS OF THIS HERE TRAIN...

NOW, BITE DOWN AND HOLD STILL IF YOU CAN...

DAMN IT! I CAIN'T DO YOU NO GOOD UP HERE.

LET ME POP OPEN A CAR AND FIGURE OUT SOME WAY TO GET YOU DOWN IN IT.

ELIJAH, YOU CAN'T JUST LEAVE ME HERE...

JEST CLOSE YOUR EYES AND I'LL BE BACK BEFORE YOU KNOW IT...

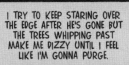

I TRY TO KEEP STARING OVER THE EDGE AFTER HE'S GONE BUT THE TREES WHIPPING PAST MAKE ME DIZZY UNTIL I FEEL LIKE I'M GONNA PURGE.

THE WIND STINGS MY EYES UNTIL I LIE ON MY BACK, WITH MY EYES CLOSED, FEELING THE RHYTHM OF RAILROAD TIE AFTER TIE PASS UNDER ME...

I THINK ABOUT MOMMA AND DADDY...

UNTIL THE VOID SWALLOWS ME WHOLE...

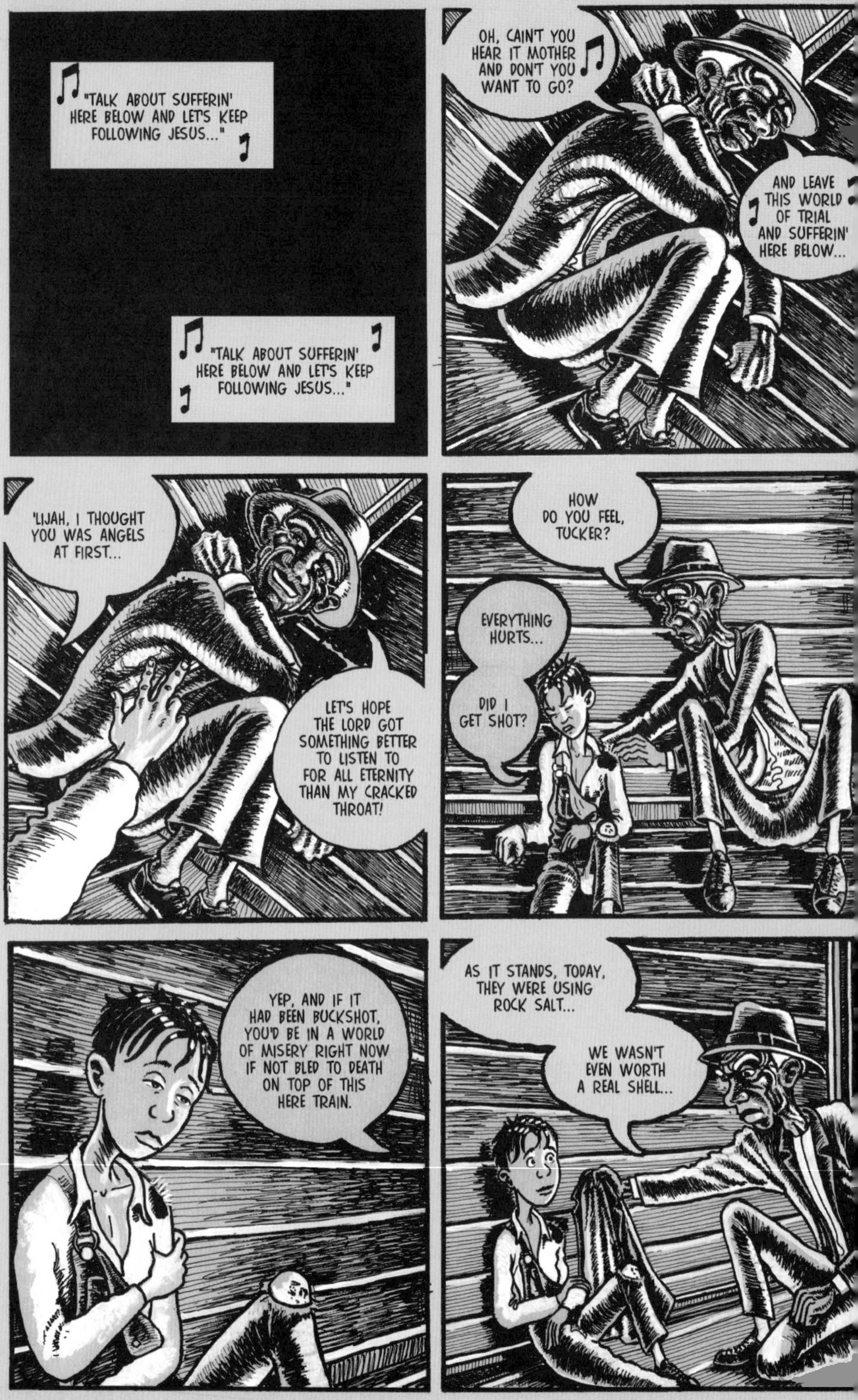
"TALK ABOUT SUFFERIN' HERE BELOW AND LET'S KEEP FOLLOWING JESUS..."
"TALK ABOUT SUFFERIN' HERE BELOW AND LET'S KEEP FOLLOWING JESUS..."
OH, CAIN'T YOU HEAR IT MOTHER AND DON'T YOU WANT TO GO?
AND LEAVE THIS WORLD OF TRIAL AND SUFFERIN' HERE BELOW...
'LIJAH, I THOUGHT YOU WAS ANGELS AT FIRST...
LET'S HOPE THE LORD GOT SOMETHING BETTER TO LISTEN TO FOR ALL ETERNITY THAN MY CRACKED THROAT!
HOW DO YOU FEEL, TUCKER?
EVERYTHING HURTS...
DID I GET SHOT?
YEP, AND IF IT HAD BEEN BUCKSHOT, YOU'D BE IN A WORLD OF MISERY RIGHT NOW IF NOT BLED TO DEATH ON TOP OF THIS HERE TRAIN.
AS IT STANDS, TODAY, THEY WERE USING ROCK SALT...
WE WASN'T EVEN WORTH A REAL SHELL...

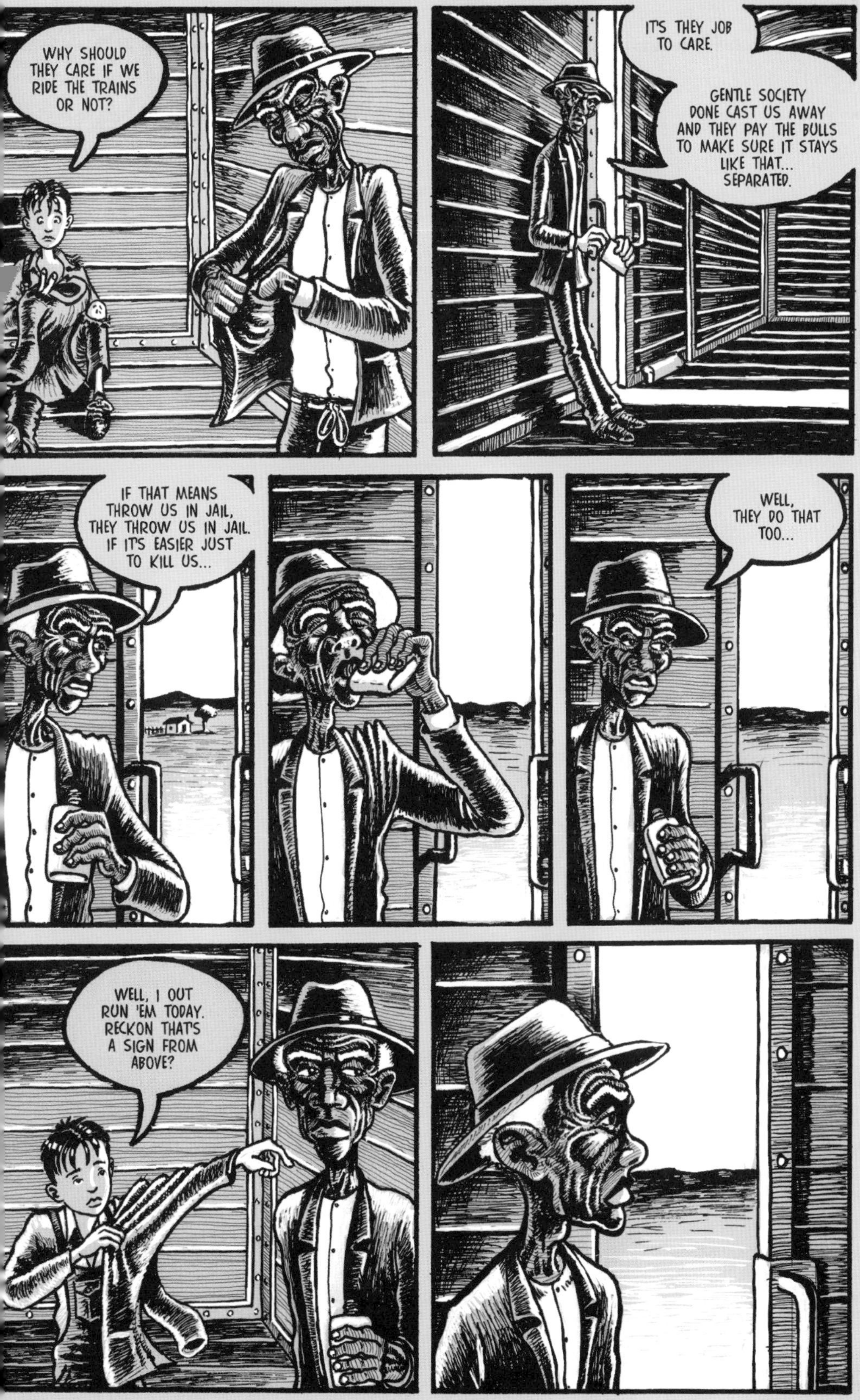
WHY SHOULD THEY CARE IF WE RIDE THE TRAINS OR NOT?
IT'S THEY JOB TO CARE.
GENTLE SOCIETY DONE CAST US AWAY AND THEY PAY THE BULLS TO MAKE SURE IT STAYS LIKE THAT... SEPARATED.
IF THAT MEANS THROW US IN JAIL, THEY THROW US IN JAIL. IF IT'S EASIER JUST TO KILL US...
WELL, THEY DO THAT TOO...
WELL, I OUT RUN 'EM TODAY. RECKON THAT'S A SIGN FROM ABOVE?

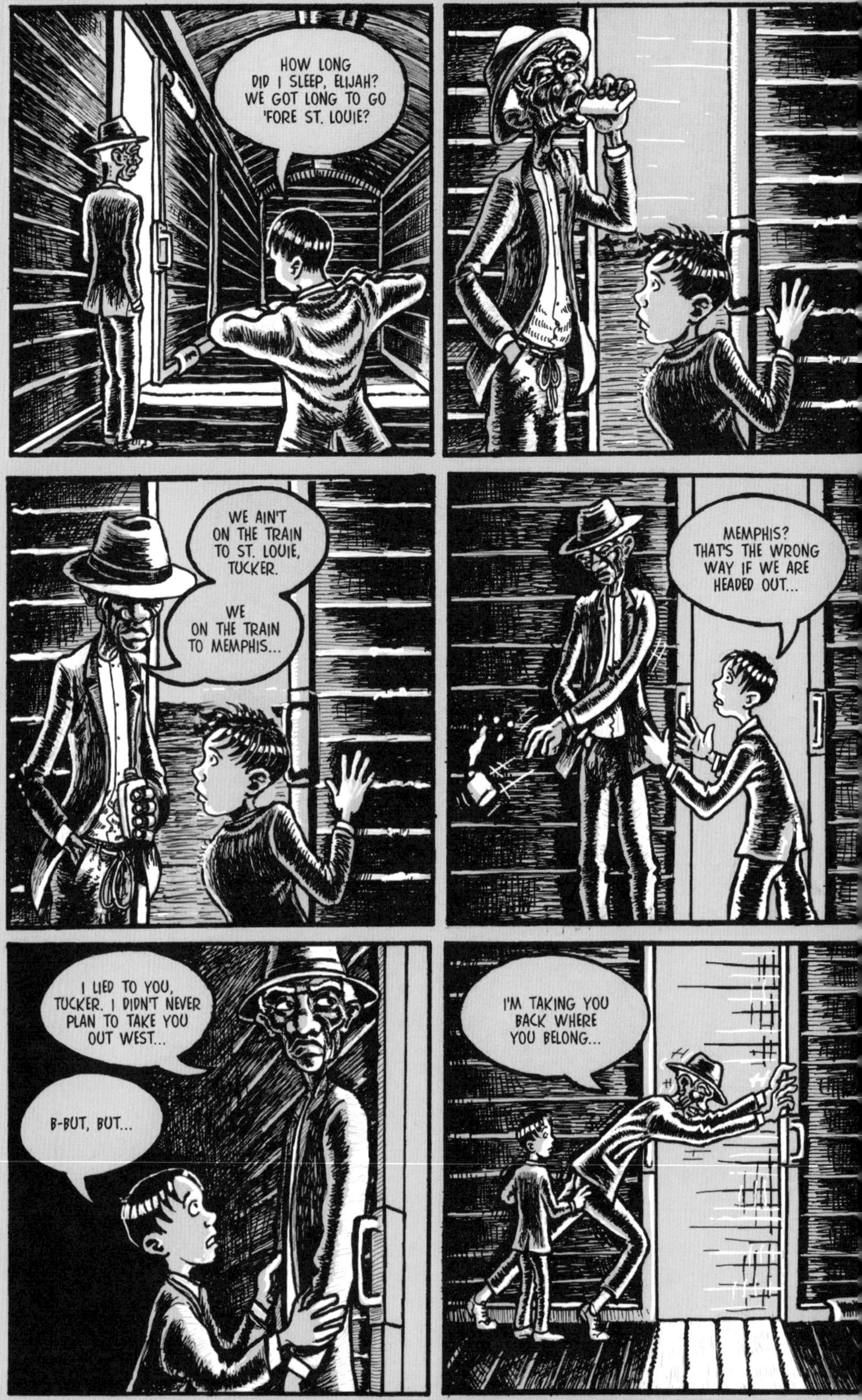
HOW LONG DID I SLEEP, ELIJAH? WE GOT LONG TO GO 'FORE ST. LOUIE?
WE AIN'T ON THE TRAIN TO ST. LOUIE, TUCKER.
WE ON THE TRAIN TO MEMPHIS...
MEMPHIS? THAT'S THE WRONG WAY IF WE ARE HEADED OUT...
I LIED TO YOU, TUCKER. I DIDN'T NEVER PLAN TO TAKE YOU OUT WEST...
B-BUT, BUT...
I'M TAKING YOU BACK WHERE YOU BELONG...

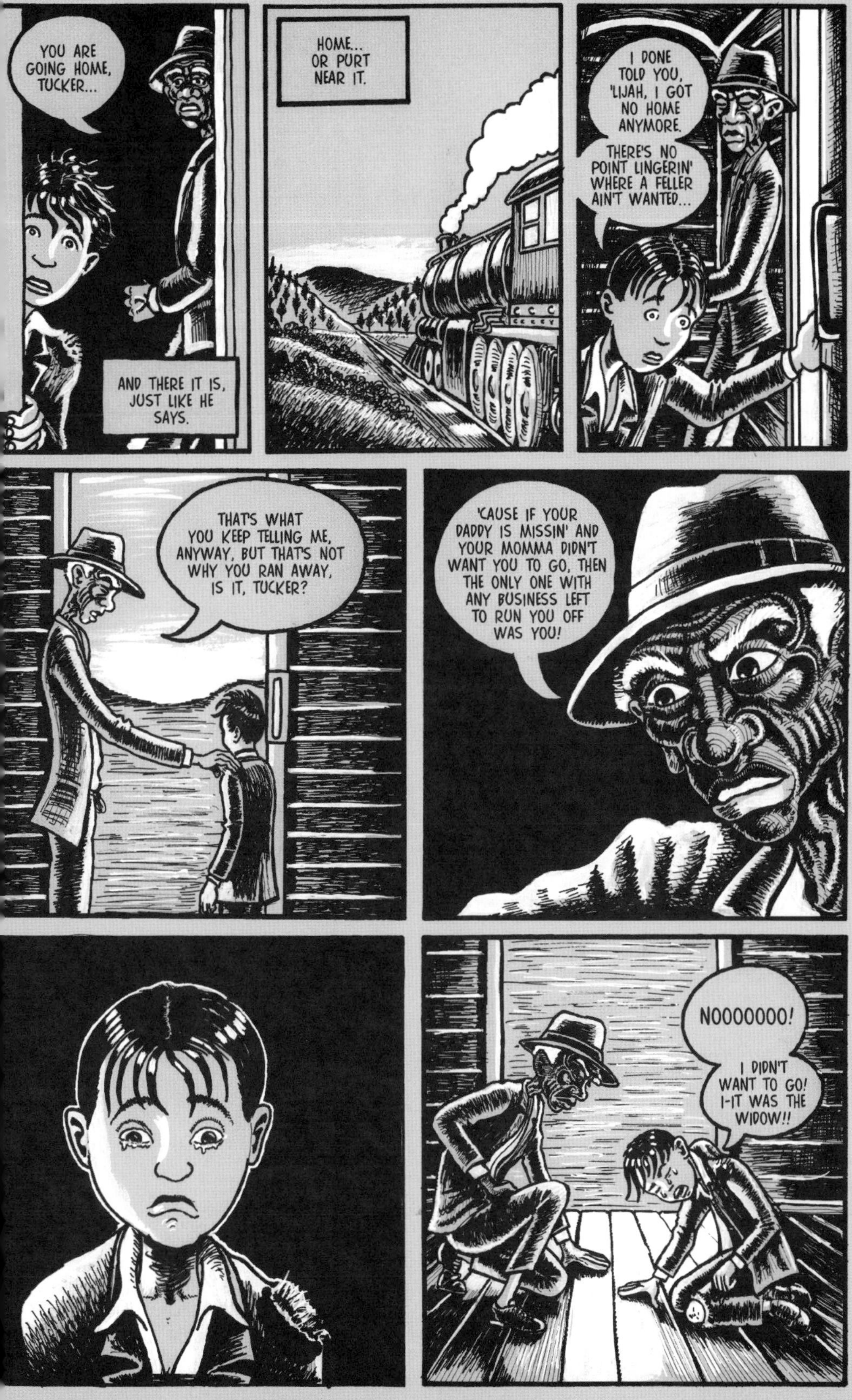

YOU ARE GOING HOME, TUCKER...
AND THERE IT IS, JUST LIKE HE SAYS.
HOME... OR PURT NEAR IT.
I DONE TOLD YOU, 'LIJAH, I GOT NO HOME ANYMORE.
THERE'S NO POINT LINGERIN' WHERE A FELLER AIN'T WANTED...
THAT'S WHAT YOU KEEP TELLING ME, ANYWAY, BUT THAT'S NOT WHY YOU RAN AWAY, IS IT, TUCKER?
'CAUSE IF YOUR DADDY IS MISSIN' AND YOUR MOMMA DIDN'T WANT YOU TO GO, THEN THE ONLY ONE WITH ANY BUSINESS LEFT TO RUN YOU OFF WAS YOU!
NOOOOOOO!
I DIDN'T WANT TO GO! I-IT WAS THE WIDOW!!

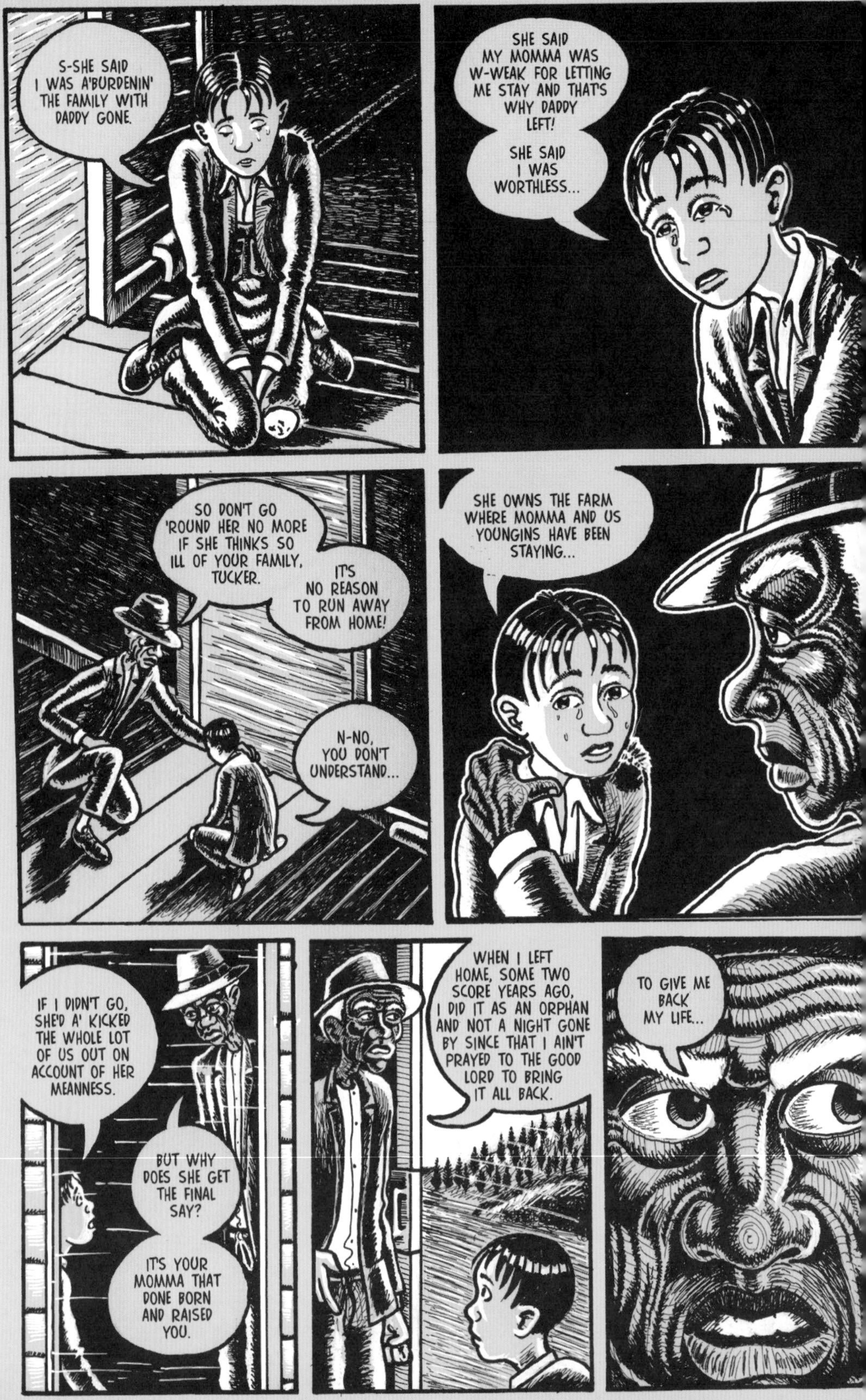
S-SHE SAID I WAS A'BURDENIN' THE FAMILY WITH DADDY GONE.
SHE SAID MY MOMMA WAS W-WEAK FOR LETTING ME STAY AND THAT'S WHY DADDY LEFT!
SHE SAID I WAS WORTHLESS...
SO DON'T GO 'ROUND HER NO MORE IF SHE THINKS SO ILL OF YOUR FAMILY, TUCKER.
IT'S NO REASON TO RUN AWAY FROM HOME!
N-NO, YOU DON'T UNDERSTAND...
SHE OWNS THE FARM WHERE MOMMA AND US YOUNGINS HAVE BEEN STAYING...
IF I DIDN'T GO, SHE'D A' KICKED THE WHOLE LOT OF US OUT ON ACCOUNT OF HER MEANNESS.
BUT WHY DOES SHE GET THE FINAL SAY?
IT'S YOUR MOMMA THAT DONE BORN AND RAISED YOU.
WHEN I LEFT HOME, SOME TWO SCORE YEARS AGO, I DID IT AS AN ORPHAN AND NOT A NIGHT GONE BY SINCE THAT I AIN'T PRAYED TO THE GOOD LORD TO BRING IT ALL BACK.
TO GIVE ME BACK MY LIFE...

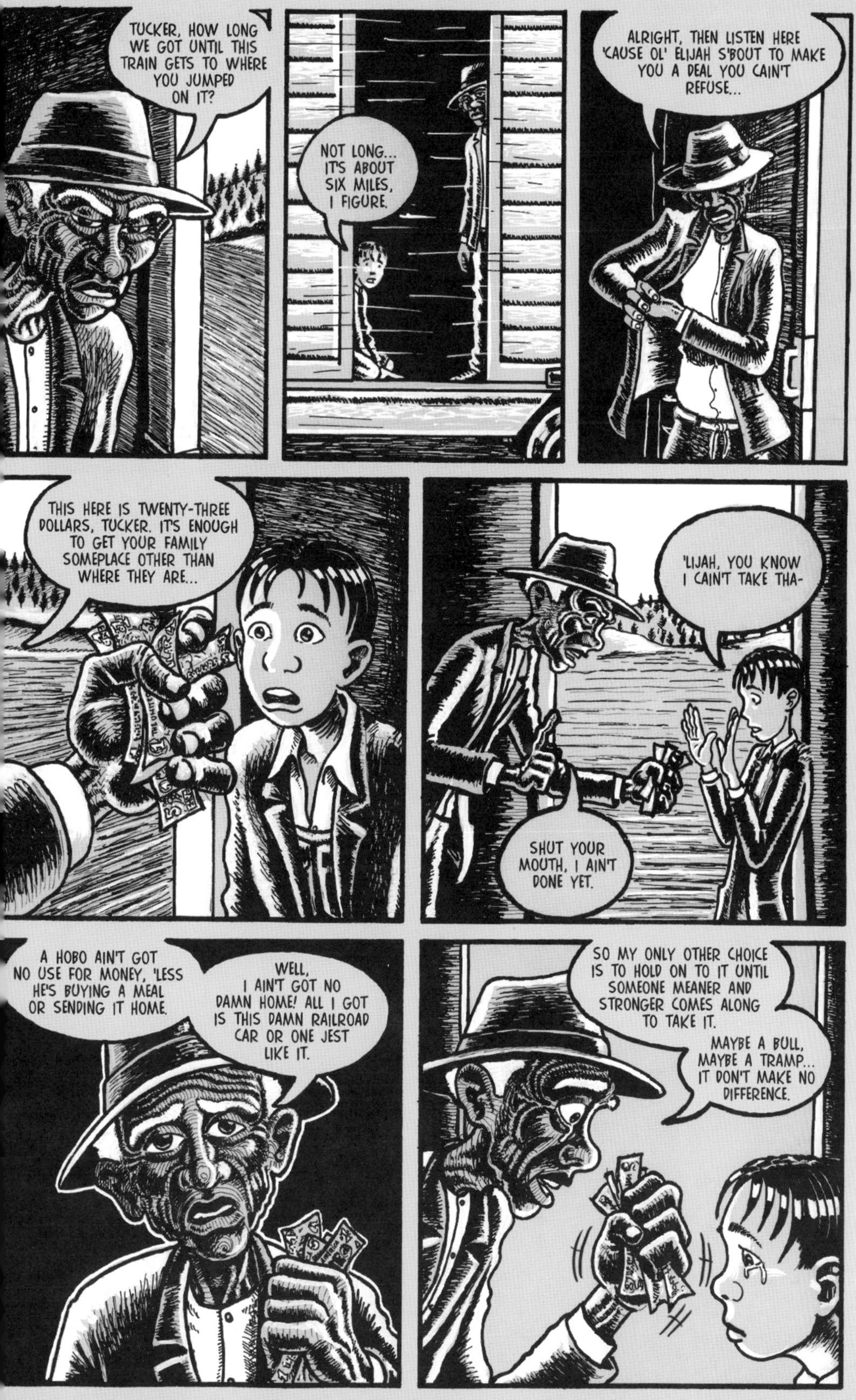

TUCKER, HOW LONG WE GOT UNTIL THIS TRAIN GETS TO WHERE YOU JUMPED ON IT?
NOT LONG... IT'S ABOUT SIX MILES, I FIGURE.
ALRIGHT, THEN LISTEN HERE 'CAUSE OL' ELIJAH S'BOUT TO MAKE YOU A DEAL YOU CAIN'T REFUSE...
THIS HERE IS TWENTY-THREE DOLLARS, TUCKER. IT'S ENOUGH TO GET YOUR FAMILY SOMEPLACE OTHER THAN WHERE THEY ARE...
'LIJAH, YOU KNOW I CAIN'T TAKE THA-
SHUT YOUR MOUTH, I AIN'T DONE YET.
A HOBO AIN'T GOT NO USE FOR MONEY, 'LESS HE'S BUYING A MEAL OR SENDING IT HOME.
WELL, I AIN'T GOT NO DAMN HOME! ALL I GOT IS THIS DAMN RAILROAD CAR OR ONE JEST LIKE IT.
SO MY ONLY OTHER CHOICE IS TO HOLD ON TO IT UNTIL SOMEONE MEANER AND STRONGER COMES ALONG TO TAKE IT.
MAYBE A BULL, MAYBE A TRAMP... IT DON'T MAKE NO DIFFERENCE.

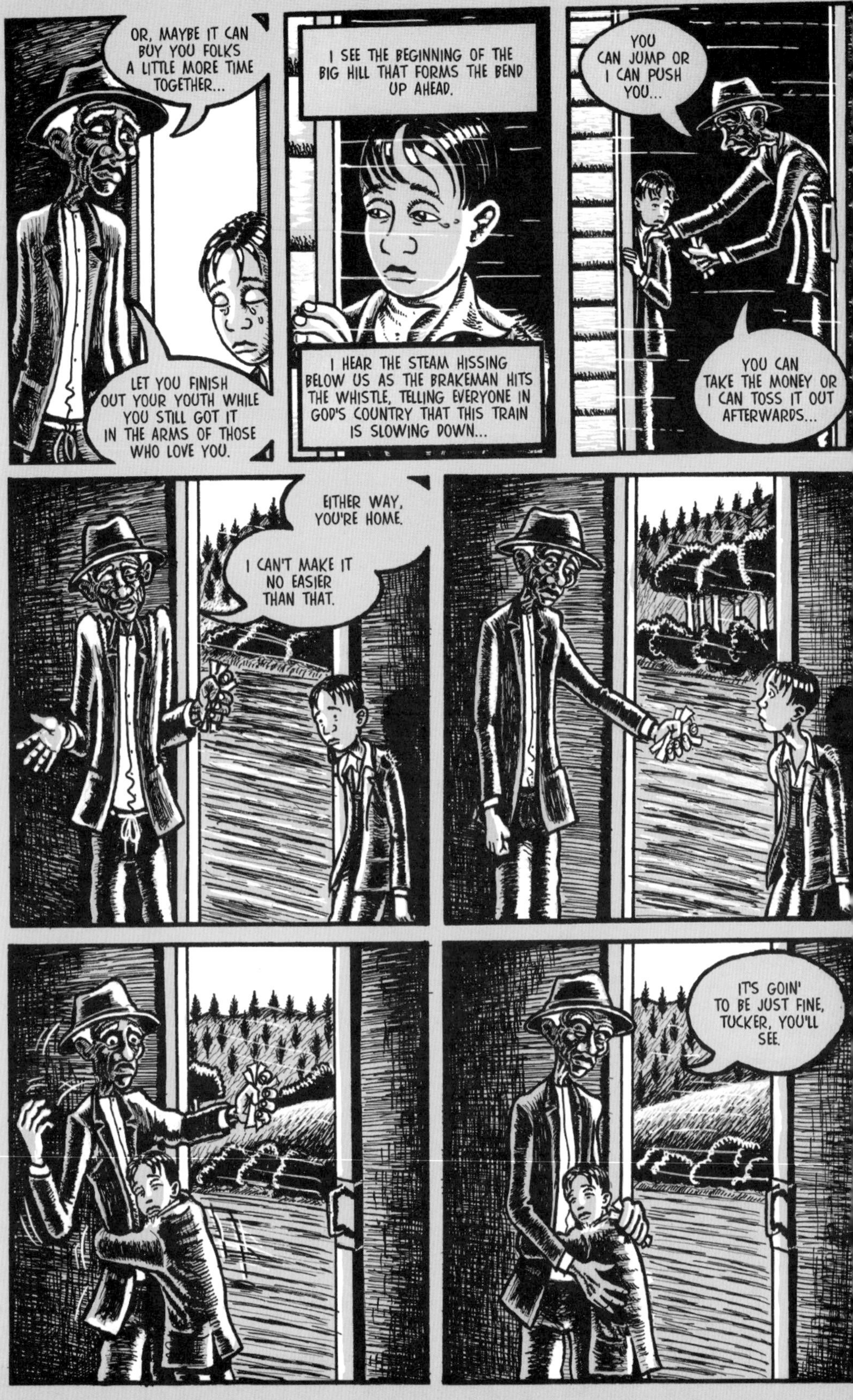
OR, MAYBE IT CAN BUY YOU FOLKS A LITTLE MORE TIME TOGETHER...
LET YOU FINISH OUT YOUR YOUTH WHILE YOU STILL GOT IT IN THE ARMS OF THOSE WHO LOVE YOU.
I SEE THE BEGINNING OF THE BIG HILL THAT FORMS THE BEND UP AHEAD.
I HEAR THE STEAM HISSING BELOW US AS THE BRAKEMAN HITS THE WHISTLE, TELLING EVERYONE IN GOD'S COUNTRY THAT THIS TRAIN IS SLOWING DOWN...
YOU CAN JUMP OR I CAN PUSH YOU...
YOU CAN TAKE THE MONEY OR I CAN TOSS IT OUT AFTERWARDS...
EITHER WAY, YOU'RE HOME.
I CAN'T MAKE IT NO EASIER THAN THAT.
IT'S GOIN' TO BE JUST FINE, TUCKER, YOU'LL SEE.

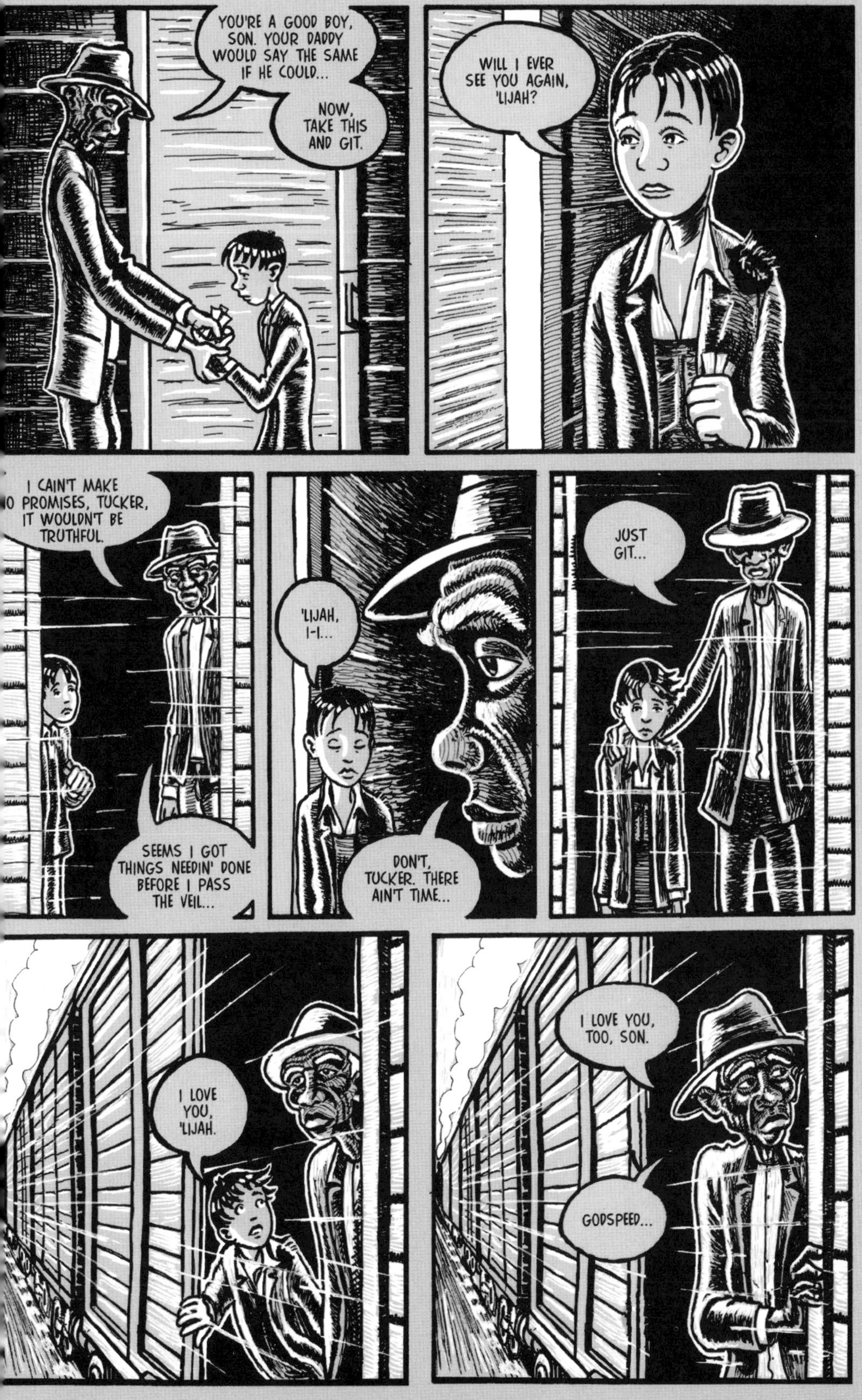
YOU'RE A GOOD BOY, SON. YOUR DADDY WOULD SAY THE SAME IF HE COULD...
NOW, TAKE THIS AND GIT.
WILL I EVER SEE YOU AGAIN, 'LIJAH?
I CAIN'T MAKE NO PROMISES, TUCKER, IT WOULDN'T BE TRUTHFUL.
SEEMS I GOT THINGS NEEDIN' DONE BEFORE I PASS THE VEIL...
'LIJAH, I-I...
DON'T, TUCKER. THERE AIN'T TIME...
JUST GIT...
I LOVE YOU, 'LIJAH.
I LOVE YOU, TOO, SON.
GODSPEED...

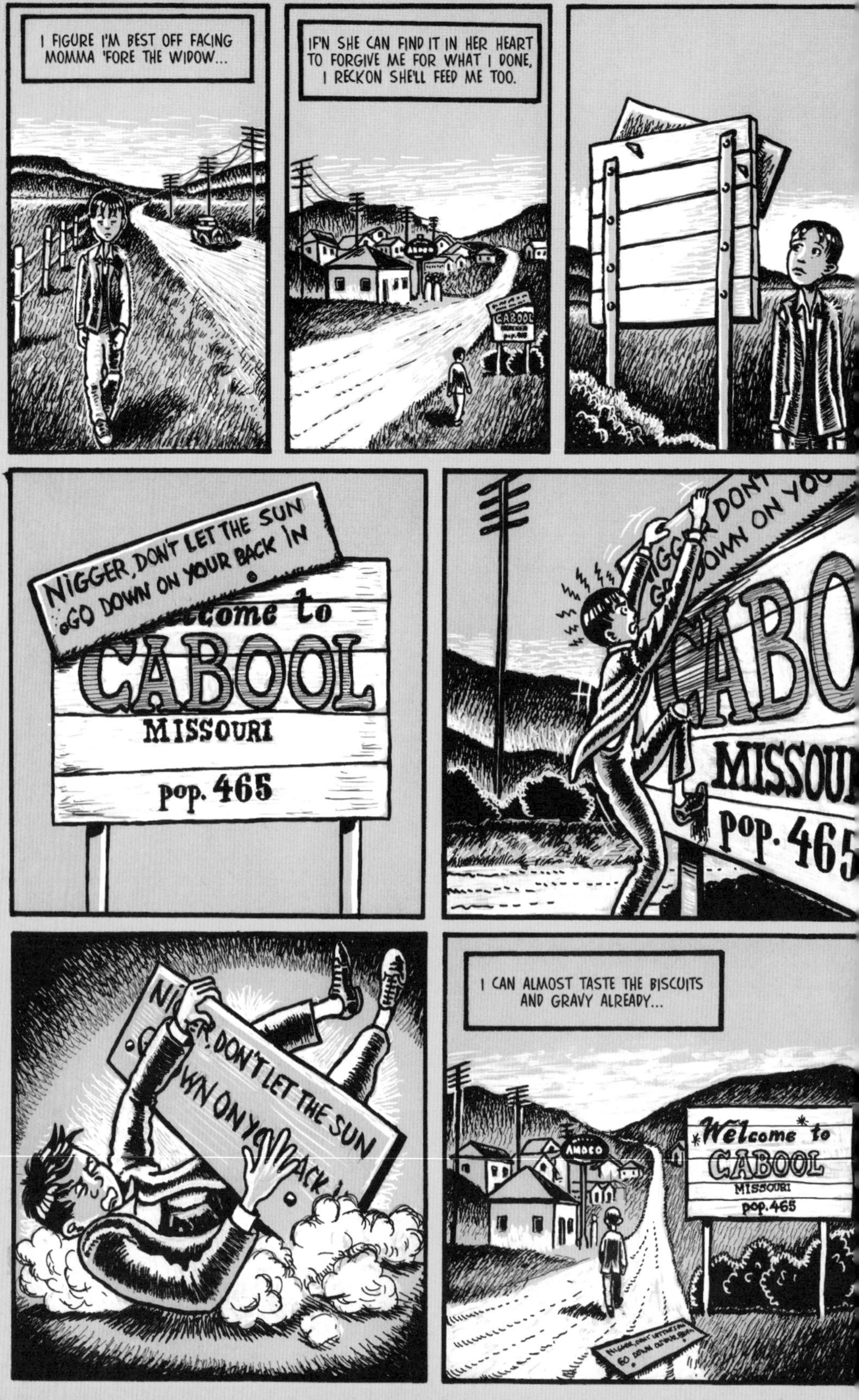
I FIGURE I'M BEST OFF FACING MOMMA 'FORE THE WIDOW...
IF'N SHE CAN FIND IT IN HER HEART TO FORGIVE ME FOR WHAT I DONE, I RECKON SHE'LL FEED ME TOO.
NIGGER, DON'T LET THE SUN GO DOWN ON YOUR BACK IN
...come to
CABOOL
MISSOURI
pop. 465
NIGGER, DON'T LET THE SUN
GO DOWN ON YOUR BACK IN
CABOO...
MISSOU...
pop. 465
NI... DON'T LET THE SUN
...WN ON YO... ACK IN
I CAN ALMOST TASTE THE BISCUITS AND GRAVY ALREADY...
AMOCO
Welcome to
CABOOL
MISSOURI
pop. 465

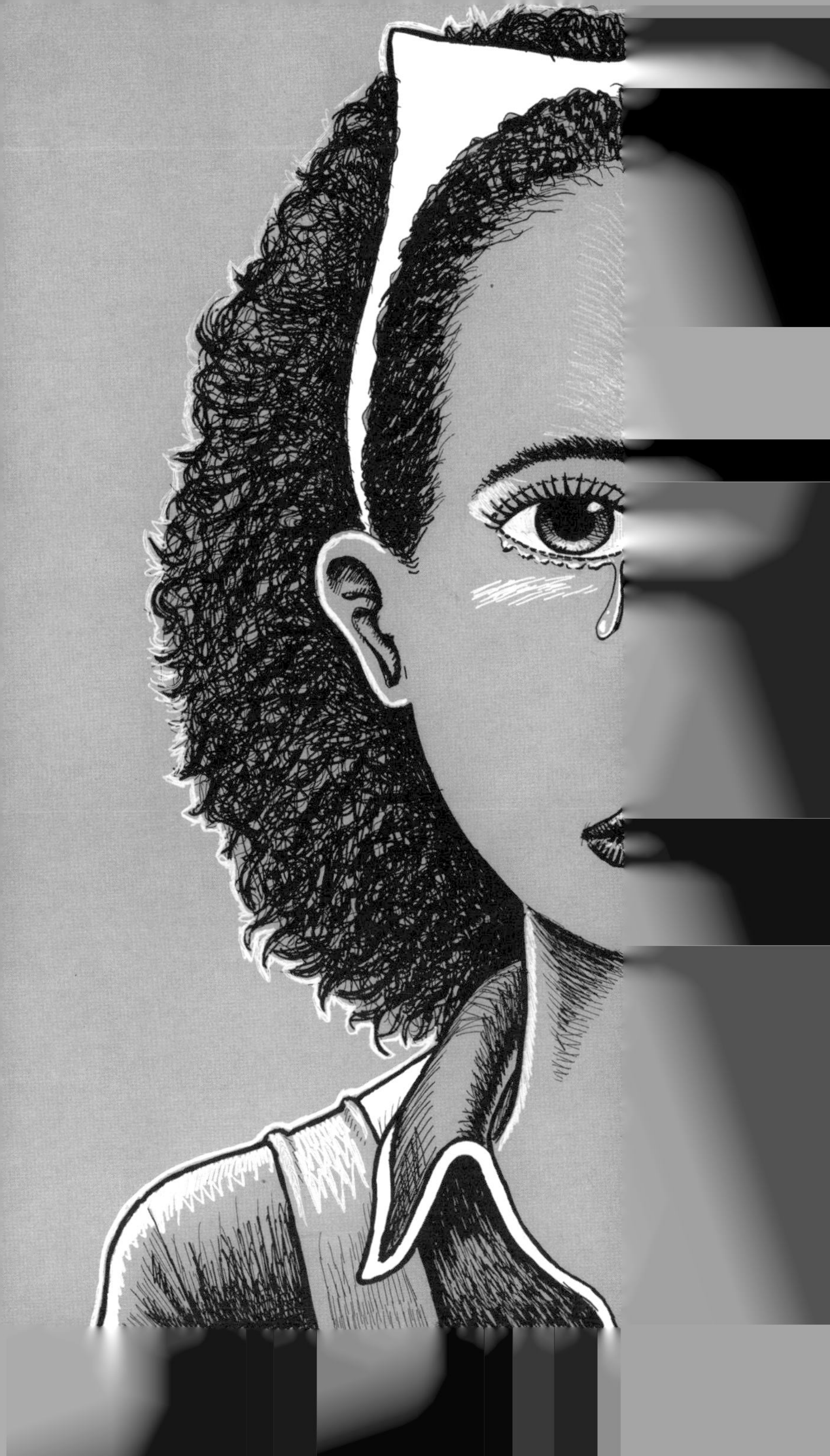

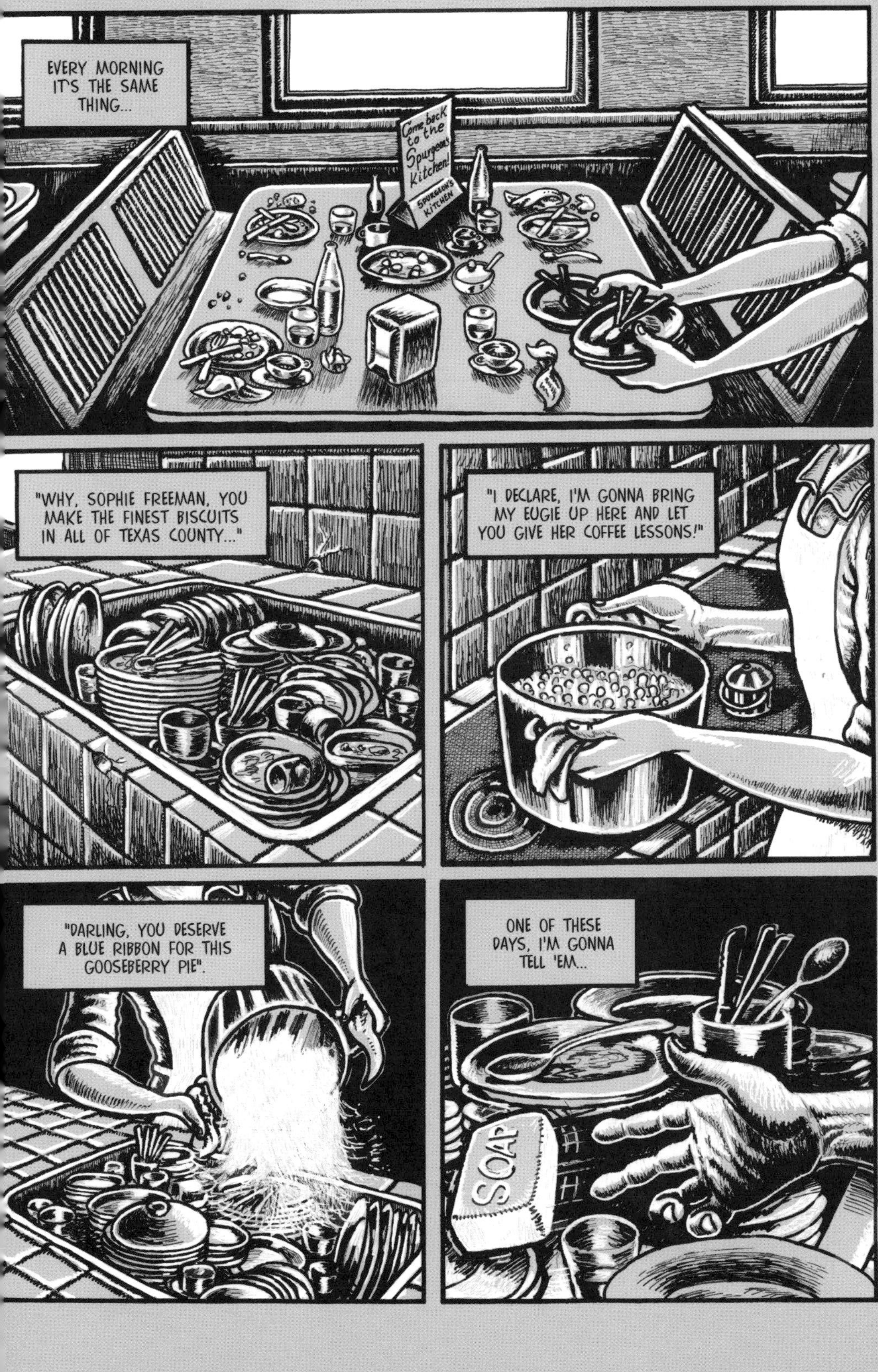
EVERY MORNING IT'S THE SAME THING...
Come back to the Spurgeon's Kitchen!
SPURGEON'S KITCHEN
"WHY, SOPHIE FREEMAN, YOU MAKE THE FINEST BISCUITS IN ALL OF TEXAS COUNTY..."
"I DECLARE, I'M GONNA BRING MY EUGIE UP HERE AND LET YOU GIVE HER COFFEE LESSONS!"
"DARLING, YOU DESERVE A BLUE RIBBON FOR THIS GOOSEBERRY PIE".
ONE OF THESE DAYS, I'M GONNA TELL 'EM...
SOAP

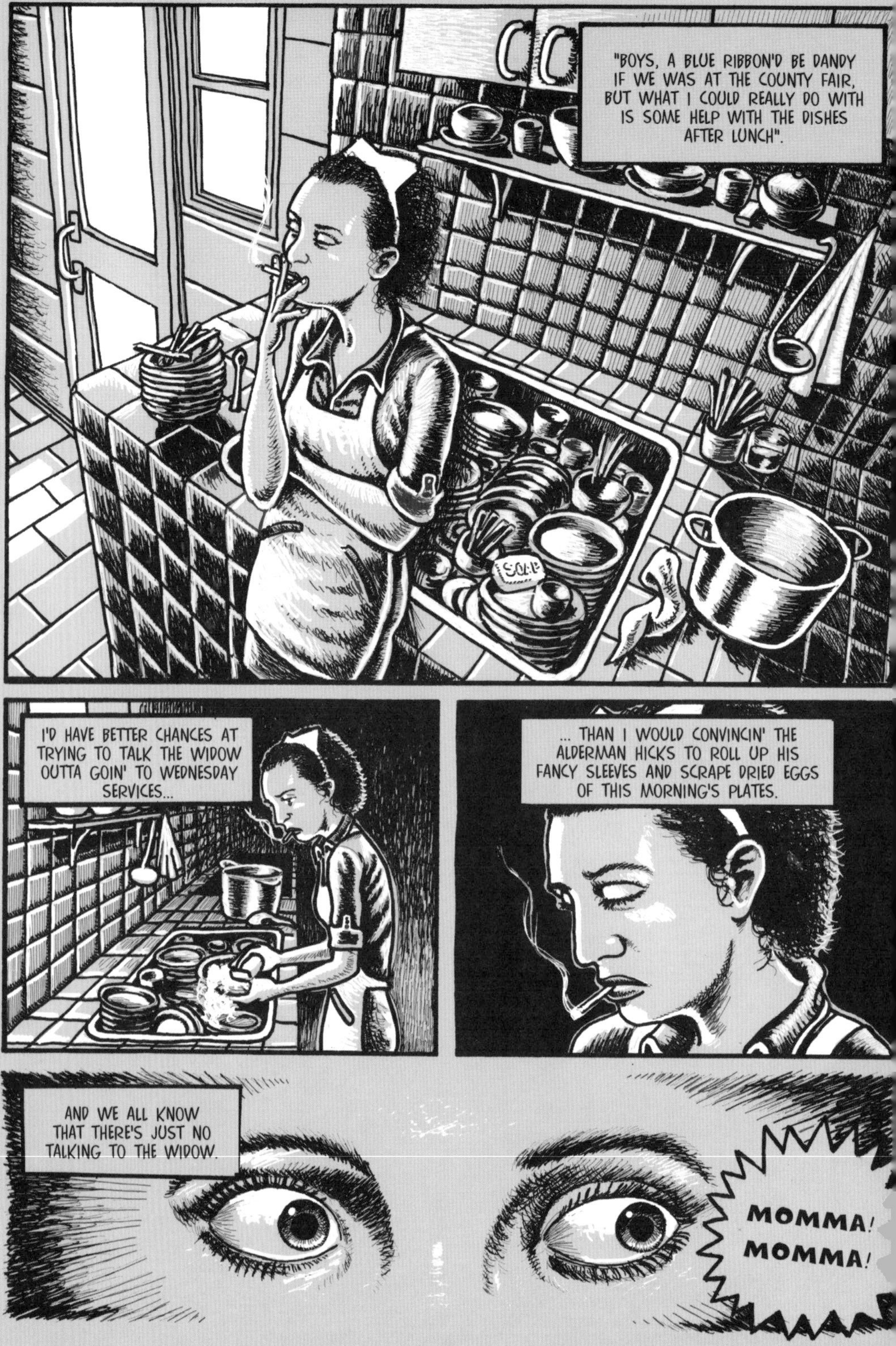
"BOYS, A BLUE RIBBON'D BE DANDY IF WE WAS AT THE COUNTY FAIR, BUT WHAT I COULD REALLY DO WITH IS SOME HELP WITH THE DISHES AFTER LUNCH".
I'D HAVE BETTER CHANCES AT TRYING TO TALK THE WIDOW OUTTA GOIN' TO WEDNESDAY SERVICES...
... THAN I WOULD CONVINCIN' THE ALDERMAN HICKS TO ROLL UP HIS FANCY SLEEVES AND SCRAPE DRIED EGGS OF THIS MORNING'S PLATES.
AND WE ALL KNOW THAT THERE'S JUST NO TALKING TO THE WIDOW.
MOMMA! MOMMA!

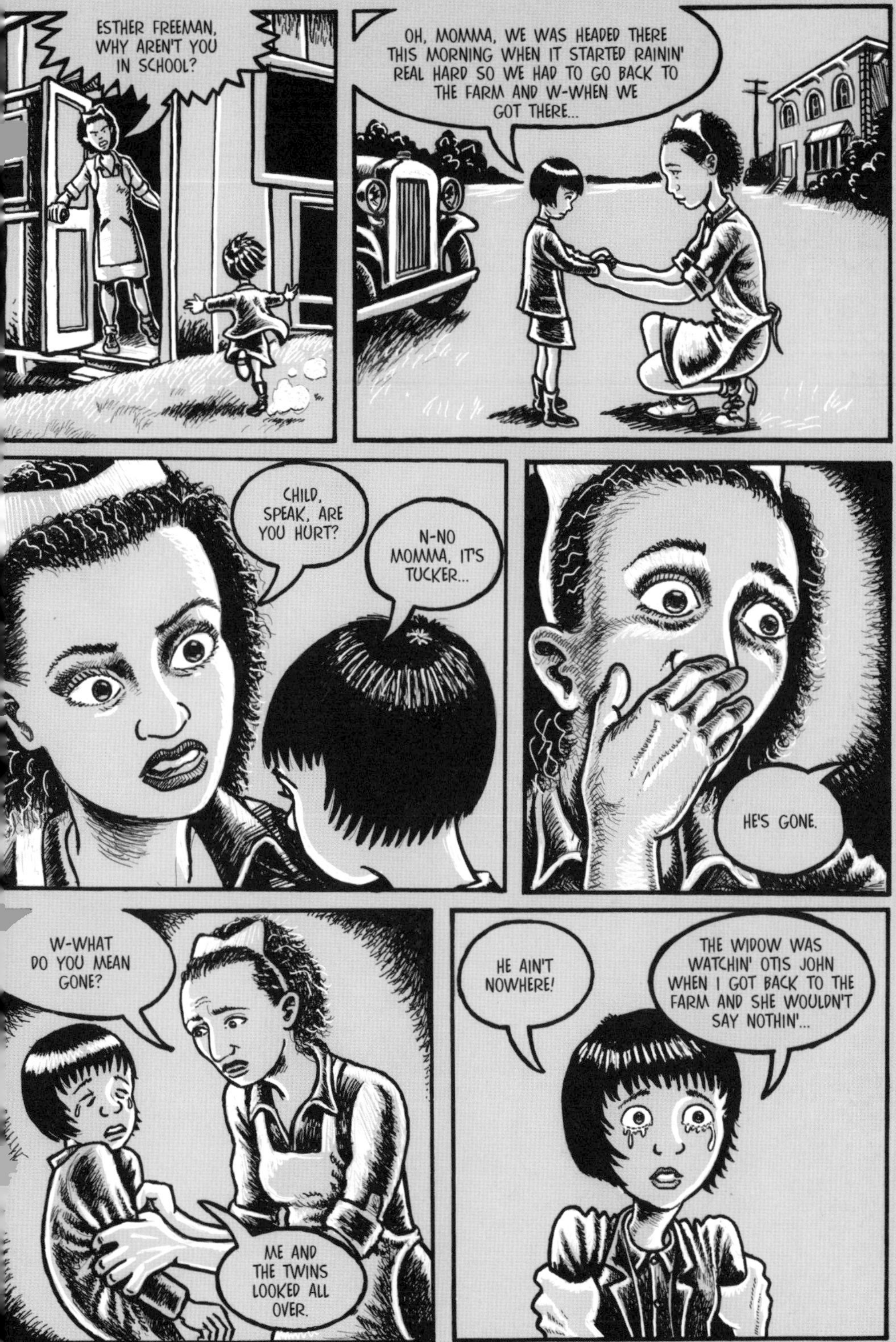
ESTHER FREEMAN, WHY AREN'T YOU IN SCHOOL?
OH, MOMMA, WE WAS HEADED THERE THIS MORNING WHEN IT STARTED RAININ' REAL HARD SO WE HAD TO GO BACK TO THE FARM AND W-WHEN WE GOT THERE...
CHILD, SPEAK, ARE YOU HURT?
N-NO MOMMA, IT'S TUCKER...
HE'S GONE.
W-WHAT DO YOU MEAN GONE?
ME AND THE TWINS LOOKED ALL OVER.
HE AIN'T NOWHERE!
THE WIDOW WAS WATCHIN' OTIS JOHN WHEN I GOT BACK TO THE FARM AND SHE WOULDN'T SAY NOTHIN'...

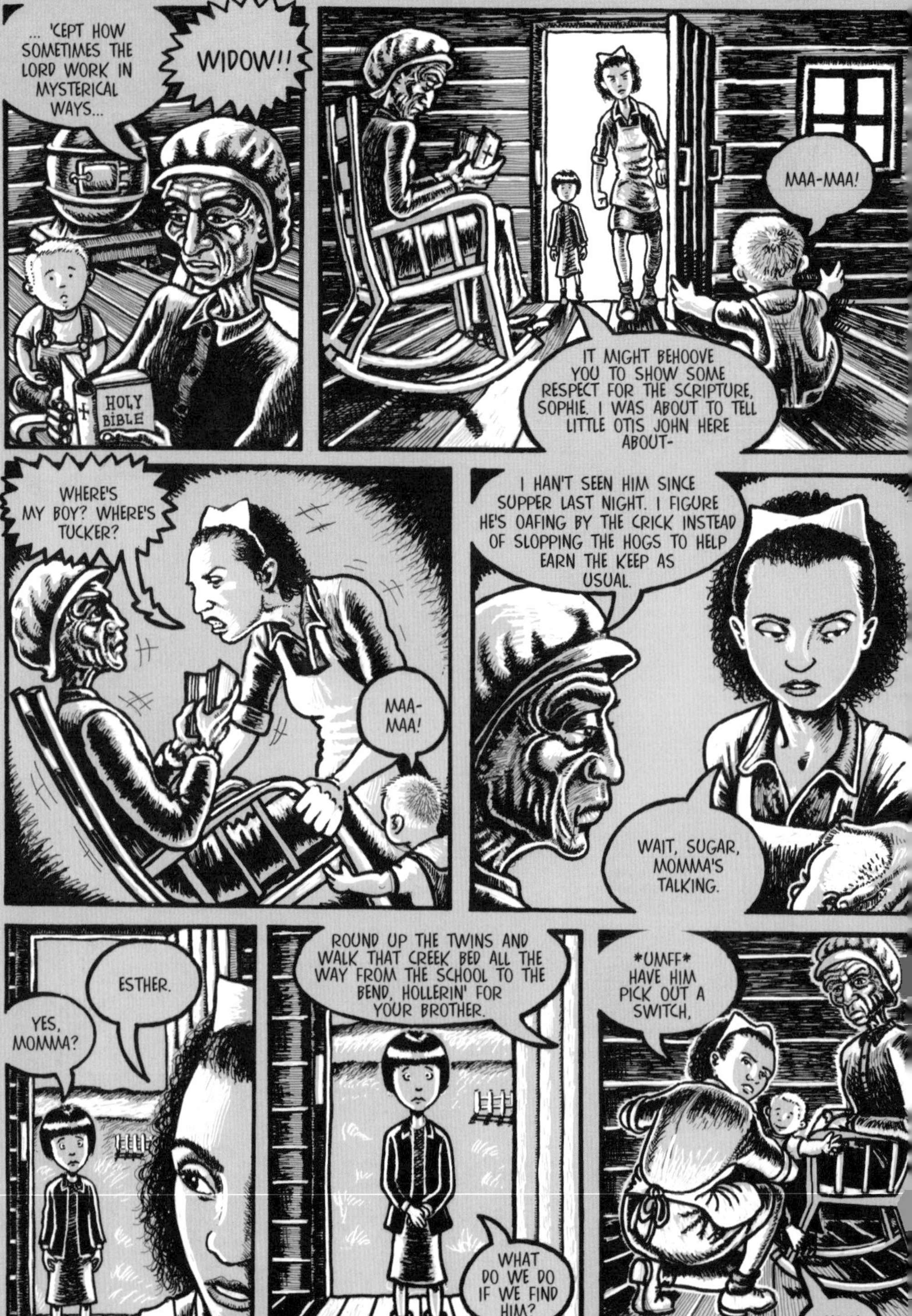
... 'CEPT HOW SOMETIMES THE LORD WORK IN MYSTERICAL WAYS...
WIDOW!!
MAA-MAA!
IT MIGHT BEHOOVE YOU TO SHOW SOME RESPECT FOR THE SCRIPTURE, SOPHIE. I WAS ABOUT TO TELL LITTLE OTIS JOHN HERE ABOUT-
HOLY BIBLE
WHERE'S MY BOY? WHERE'S TUCKER?
MAA-MAA!
I HAN'T SEEN HIM SINCE SUPPER LAST NIGHT. I FIGURE HE'S OAFING BY THE CRICK INSTEAD OF SLOPPING THE HOGS TO HELP EARN THE KEEP AS USUAL.
WAIT, SUGAR, MOMMA'S TALKING.
ESTHER.
YES, MOMMA?
ROUND UP THE TWINS AND WALK THAT CREEK BED ALL THE WAY FROM THE SCHOOL TO THE BEND, HOLLERIN' FOR YOUR BROTHER.
WHAT DO WE DO IF WE FIND HIM?
UMFF HAVE HIM PICK OUT A SWITCH,
NOW GIT!

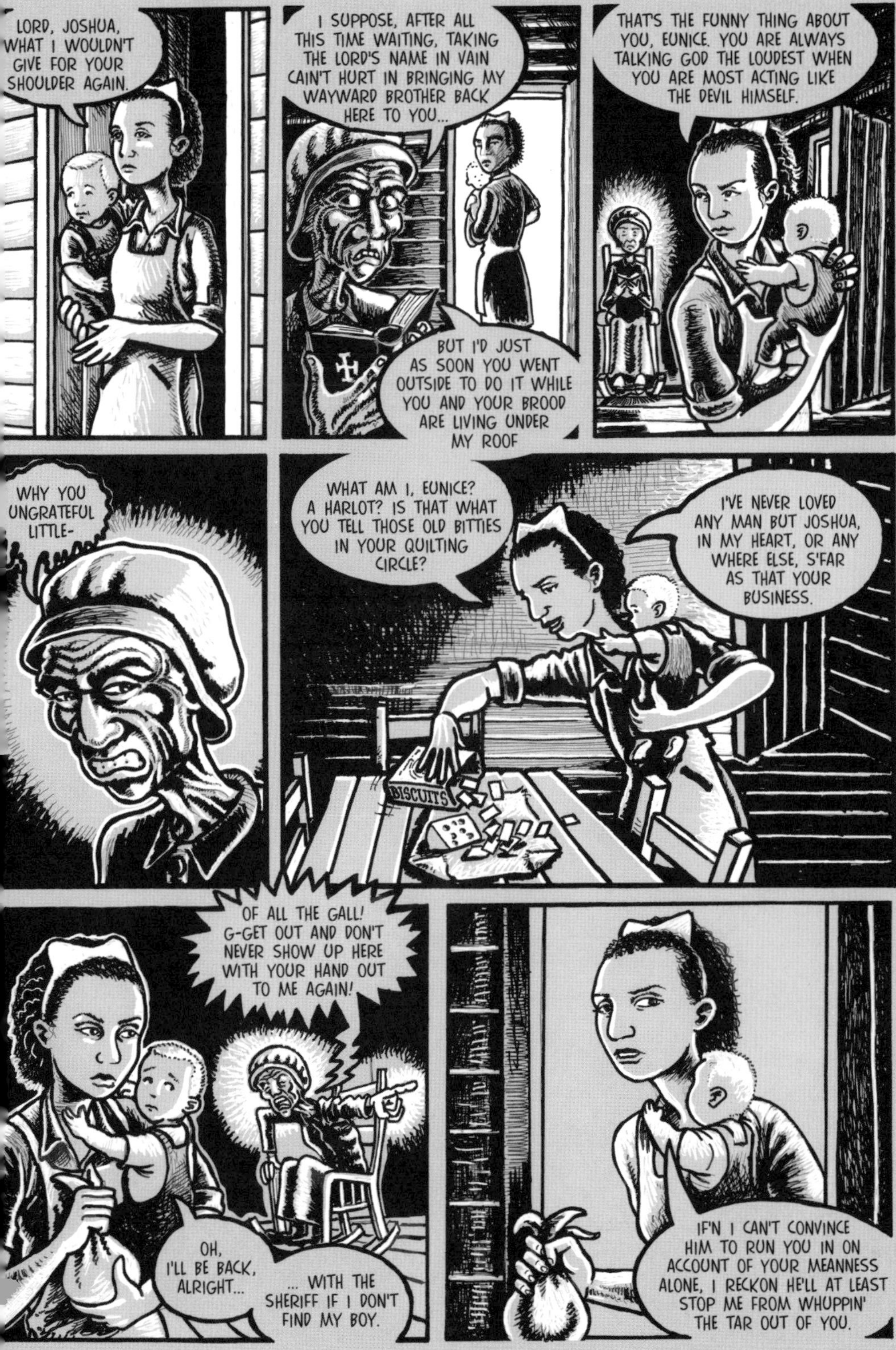
LORD, JOSHUA, WHAT I WOULDN'T GIVE FOR YOUR SHOULDER AGAIN.
I SUPPOSE, AFTER ALL THIS TIME WAITING, TAKING THE LORD'S NAME IN VAIN CAIN'T HURT IN BRINGING MY WAYWARD BROTHER BACK HERE TO YOU...
BUT I'D JUST AS SOON YOU WENT OUTSIDE TO DO IT WHILE YOU AND YOUR BROOD ARE LIVING UNDER MY ROOF
THAT'S THE FUNNY THING ABOUT YOU, EUNICE. YOU ARE ALWAYS TALKING GOD THE LOUDEST WHEN YOU ARE MOST ACTING LIKE THE DEVIL HIMSELF.
WHY YOU UNGRATEFUL LITTLE-
WHAT AM I, EUNICE? A HARLOT? IS THAT WHAT YOU TELL THOSE OLD BITTIES IN YOUR QUILTING CIRCLE?
I'VE NEVER LOVED ANY MAN BUT JOSHUA, IN MY HEART, OR ANY WHERE ELSE, S'FAR AS THAT YOUR BUSINESS.
BISCUITS
OF ALL THE GALL! G-GET OUT AND DON'T NEVER SHOW UP HERE WITH YOUR HAND OUT TO ME AGAIN!
OH, I'LL BE BACK, ALRIGHT...
... WITH THE SHERIFF IF I DON'T FIND MY BOY.
IF'N I CAN'T CONVINCE HIM TO RUN YOU IN ON ACCOUNT OF YOUR MEANNESS ALONE, I RECKON HE'LL AT LEAST STOP ME FROM WHUPPIN' THE TAR OUT OF YOU.

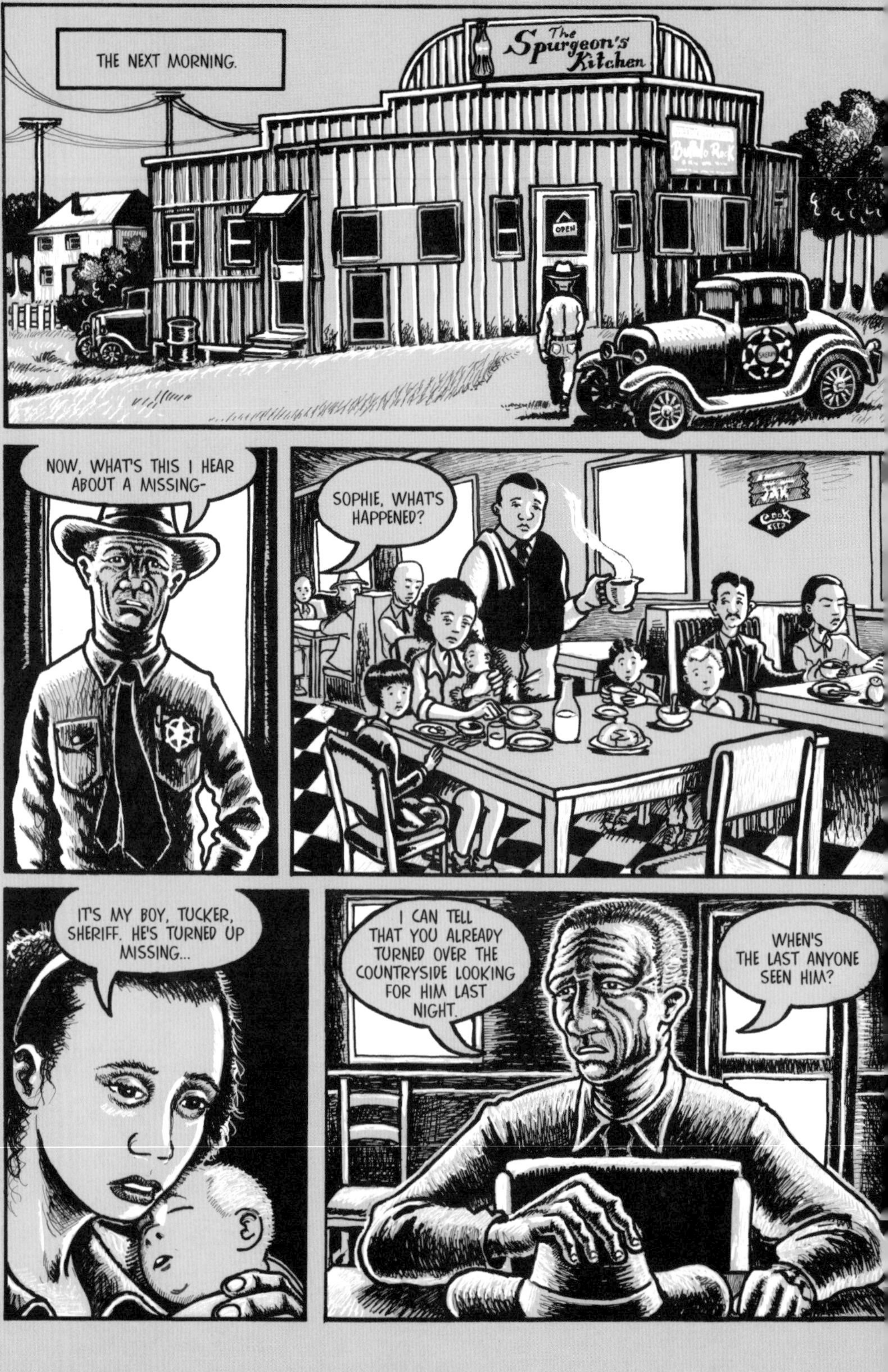
THE NEXT MORNING.
The Spurgeon's Kitchen
OPEN
NOW, WHAT'S THIS I HEAR ABOUT A MISSING-
SOPHIE, WHAT'S HAPPENED?
IT'S MY BOY, TUCKER, SHERIFF. HE'S TURNED UP MISSING...
I CAN TELL THAT YOU ALREADY TURNED OVER THE COUNTRYSIDE LOOKING FOR HIM LAST NIGHT.
WHEN'S THE LAST ANYONE SEEN HIM?

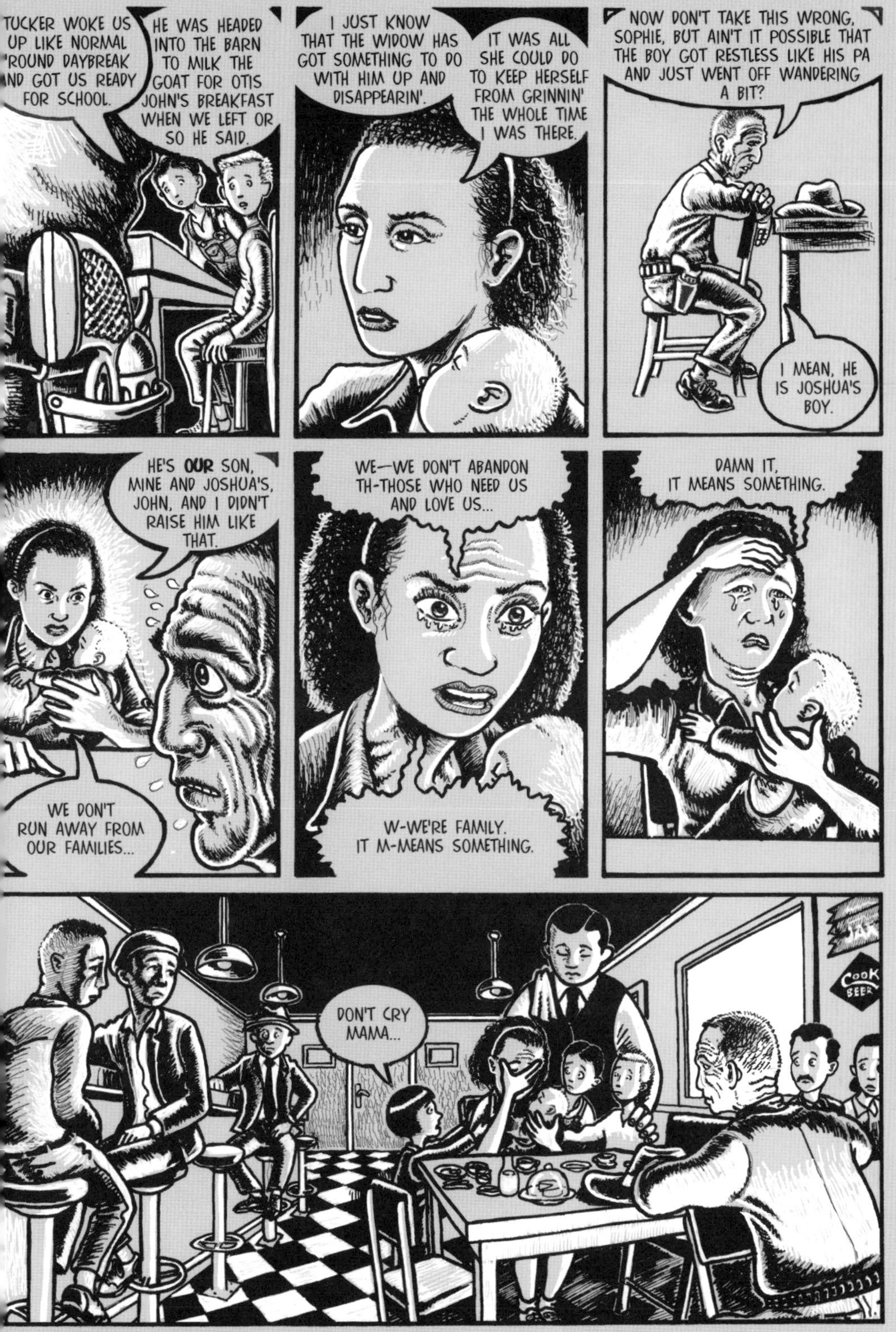
TUCKER WOKE US UP LIKE NORMAL 'ROUND DAYBREAK AND GOT US READY FOR SCHOOL.
HE WAS HEADED INTO THE BARN TO MILK THE GOAT FOR OTIS JOHN'S BREAKFAST WHEN WE LEFT OR SO HE SAID.
I JUST KNOW THAT THE WIDOW HAS GOT SOMETHING TO DO WITH HIM UP AND DISAPPEARIN'.
IT WAS ALL SHE COULD DO TO KEEP HERSELF FROM GRINNIN' THE WHOLE TIME I WAS THERE.
NOW DON'T TAKE THIS WRONG, SOPHIE, BUT AIN'T IT POSSIBLE THAT THE BOY GOT RESTLESS LIKE HIS PA AND JUST WENT OFF WANDERING A BIT?
I MEAN, HE IS JOSHUA'S BOY.
HE'S **OUR** SON, MINE AND JOSHUA'S, JOHN, AND I DIDN'T RAISE HIM LIKE THAT.
WE DON'T RUN AWAY FROM OUR FAMILIES...
WE—WE DON'T ABANDON TH-THOSE WHO NEED US AND LOVE US...
W-WE'RE FAMILY. IT M-MEANS SOMETHING.
DAMN IT, IT MEANS SOMETHING.
DON'T CRY MAMA...
COOK BEER

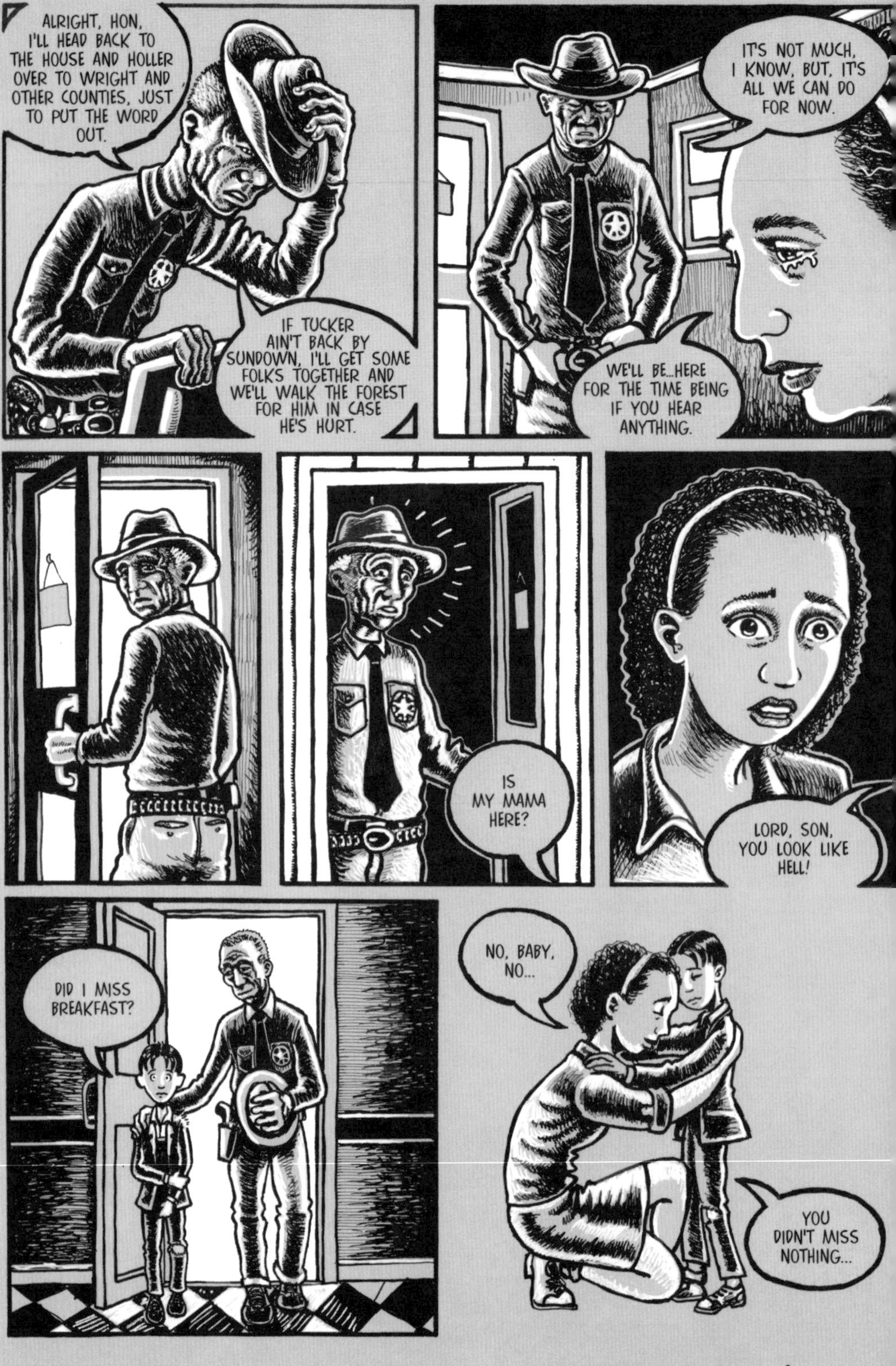
ALRIGHT, HON, I'LL HEAD BACK TO THE HOUSE AND HOLLER OVER TO WRIGHT AND OTHER COUNTIES, JUST TO PUT THE WORD OUT.
IF TUCKER AIN'T BACK BY SUNDOWN, I'LL GET SOME FOLKS TOGETHER AND WE'LL WALK THE FOREST FOR HIM IN CASE HE'S HURT.
IT'S NOT MUCH, I KNOW, BUT, IT'S ALL WE CAN DO FOR NOW.
WE'LL BE...HERE FOR THE TIME BEING IF YOU HEAR ANYTHING.
IS MY MAMA HERE?
LORD, SON, YOU LOOK LIKE HELL!
DID I MISS BREAKFAST?
NO, BABY, NO...
YOU DIDN'T MISS NOTHING...

End

EPILOGUE

The story that you have just read (or are considering reading in skimming this here epilogue to see if we are your kind of folks) is a work of fiction. To the best of my knowledge, no one ever tore down that hateful sign that was posted on the outskirts of Cabool, Missouri (and many other towns) until it was finally taken down for good...a date that eluded my own research on the topic.

But, it was definitely there and, as a result, just like Tucker, my grandmother, Ruth Marie Bradley, who was born and lived in Cabool, did not, by her own admission, even meet a person of African-American descent until she was in her twenties (the 1950s). Lucky for me, her natural sense of tolerance was well-developed by that time from years of hard but honest living, not only making do with which she had, but also providing for others. In time, she instilled in my mother those same values and so, for reasons too diverse for breezy consideration and fates too kind for scrutiny, I was raised among the well-publicized intolerance and occasional willful ignorance of the Mid-South with a hand taught to shake, not to make a fist. My grandmother also shared stories with me about her childhood, stories that would eventually settle into myth after we left the countryside for the city during the lean Reagan years. Her father was, in addition to being a war veteran and a dedicated provider for his family, a hobo. He was a migrant worker, distinguished from the immigrant populations that still work those same lush California fields today only by time and casual ethnicity. This lifestyle, of riding the rails to get to where the work was, was common to many uneducated men from all over the region and wouldn't, until the Great Depression, guarantee a feller a bad lot for himself, either, if he was diligent.

JAX
GUS CAFE
Hot Cakes and
Cofee 10c
Stew 10c
Hamburgers 5c
6 for 25c

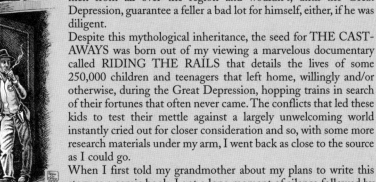

Despite this mythological inheritance, the seed for THE CASTAWAYS was born out of my viewing a marvelous documentary called RIDING THE RAILS that details the lives of some 250,000 children and teenagers that left home, willingly and/or otherwise, during the Great Depression, hopping trains in search of their fortunes that often never came. The conflicts that led these kids to test their mettle against a largely unwelcoming world instantly cried out for closer consideration and so, with some more research materials under my arm, I went back as close to the source as I could go.

When I first told my grandmother about my plans to write this story as a comic book, I got a long moment of silence followed by her perfunctory, "Well, Gawd..."

But, she quickly warmed up to my incessant questions about "the old days," reveling, maybe for the first time, in the chance to tell her story, one she often commented on as being dull or somehow without merit before losing herself again in enthusiastic reminiscence. I kept taking notes. One day while we were talking, I was frothing at the mouth about the socio-economic conditions in the rural South during the late Twenties when Grandma stopped me short, asking, "Robbie, why was Daddy gone so much when I was small?" I stammered for a moment before finally settling on, "It was the only way he knew how to make money when times got hard."

Strangely, she seemed satisfied enough with that, as if I had somehow answered a question that had been on her mind for a very long time. I'm not even sure that what I said was as important as the fact that someone had finally recognized her loss.

Less than a year later, three months before the first serialized installment of THE CASTAWAYS was due to hit the shelves, Ruthie was overcome by an aggressive brain tumor and, after a month of fighting, she finally passed the veil in my home, surrounded by her family.

I remember at one point in her struggle, she swam up to consciousness from beneath the sea of morphia to tell us that a black man had been there and he was going to take her to St. Louis. Distracted as I was at the time by my own intense grief, I didn't see the connection between her vision and the story I was writing, largely drawn from the fertile soil of her life but now, in reflection, maybe I understand.

I can only hope that Elijah put her on the train to Memphis, instead, so she could get back home...where she belonged.

Thank you again for your kind patronage. Y'all come back now, you hear?

ROB VOLLMAR

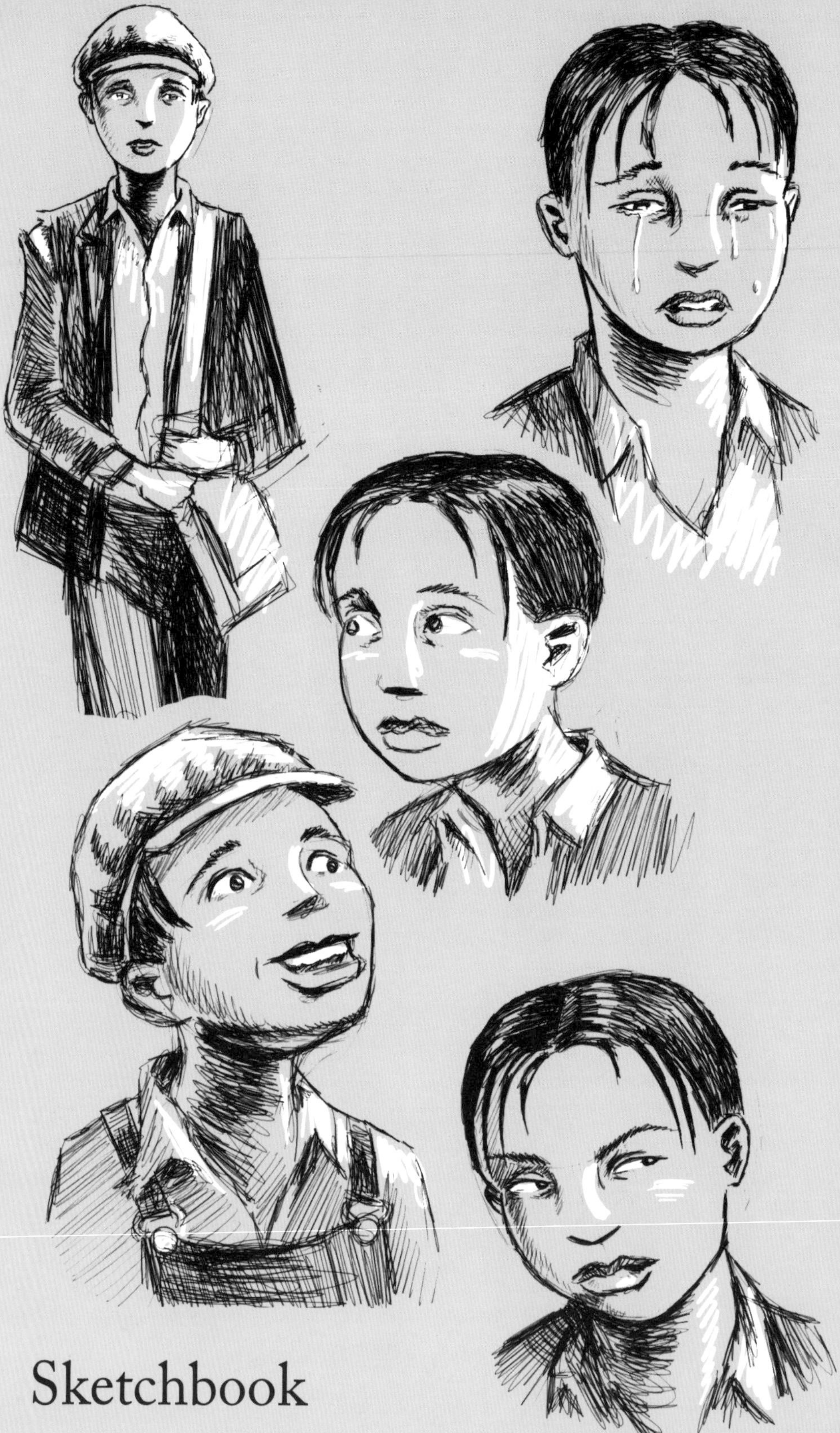

Sketchbook

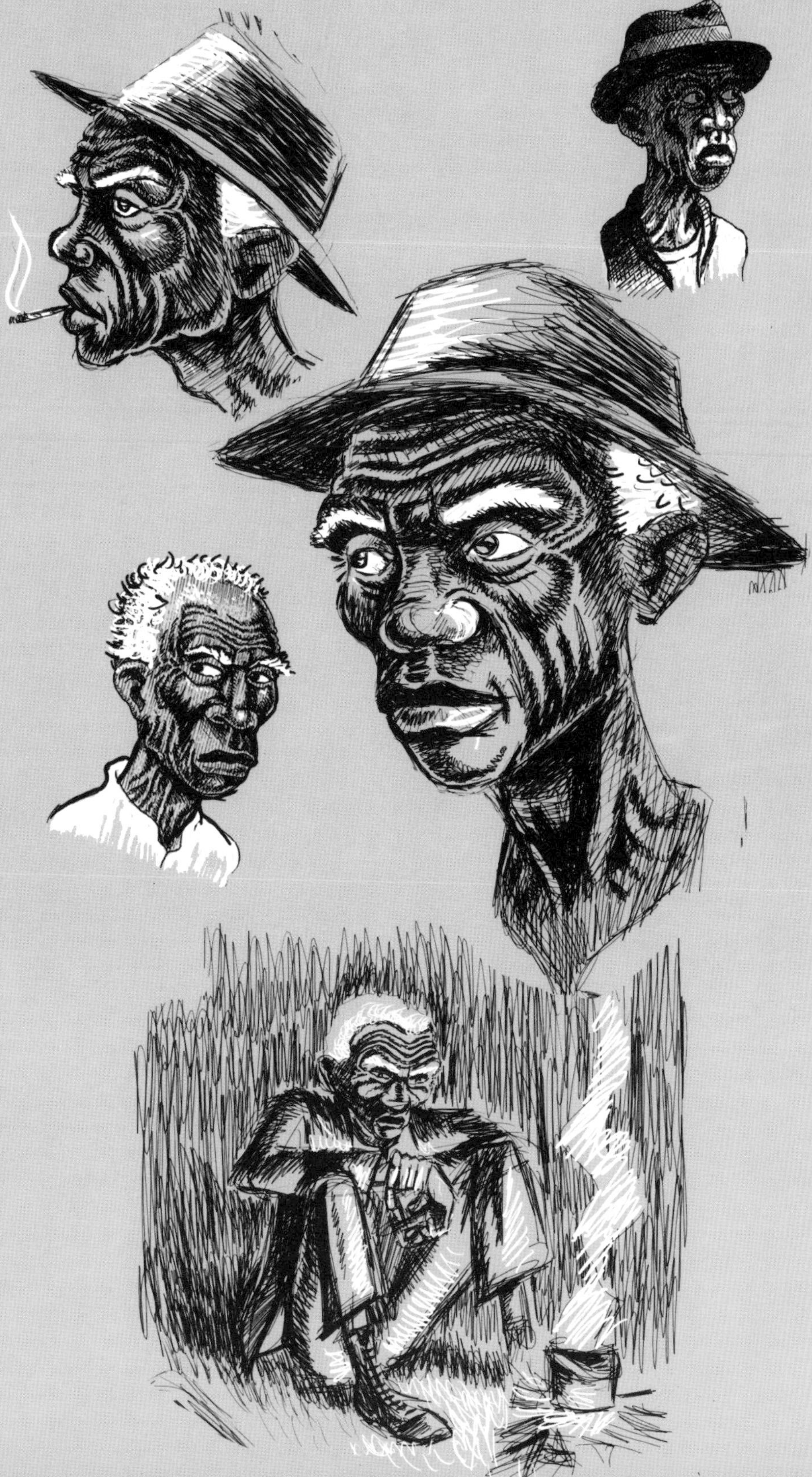

Sept. 2008

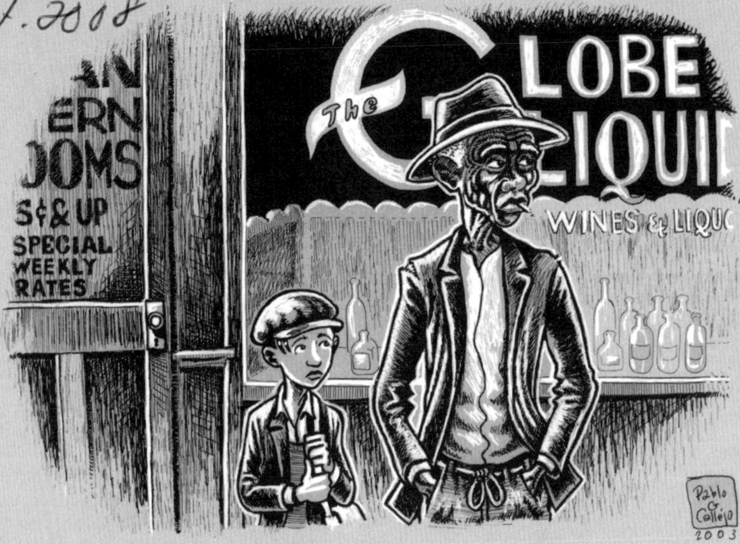

AN
ERN
OOMS
S¢& UP
SPECIAL
WEEKLY
RATES
The
LOBE
LIQUI
WINES & LIQU
Pablo G. Callejo
2003

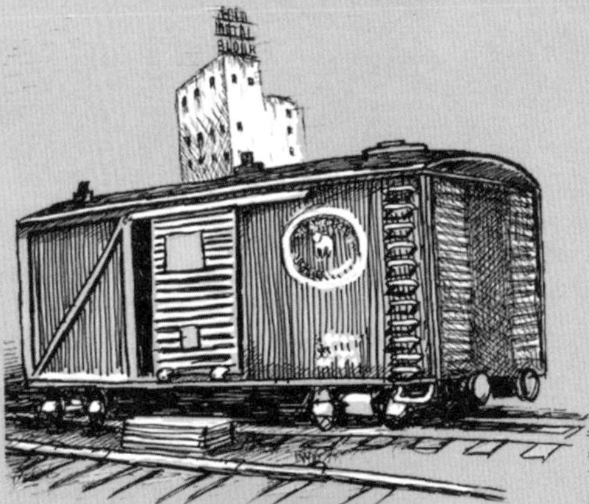

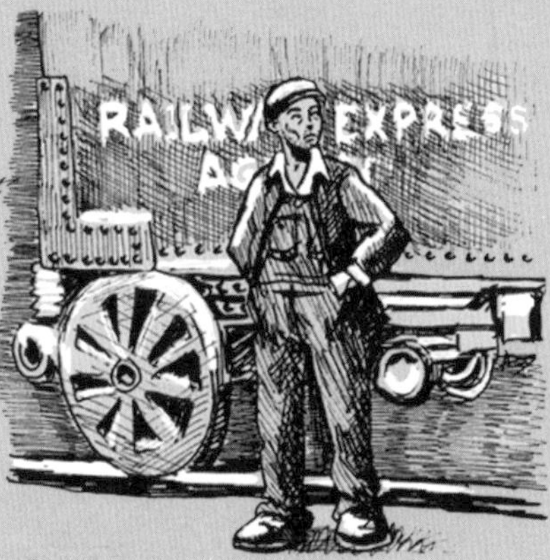

RAILW EXPRESS

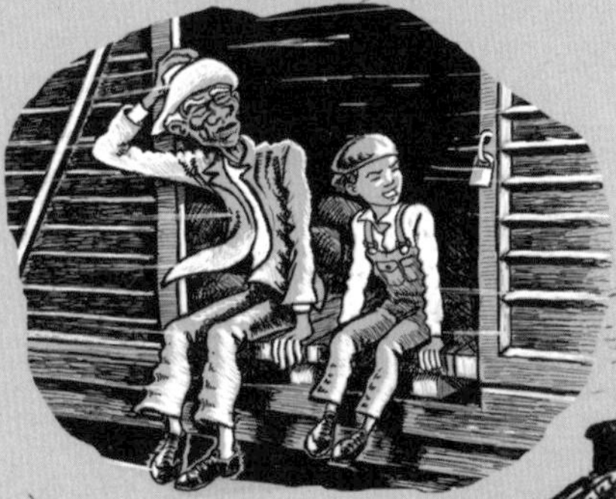

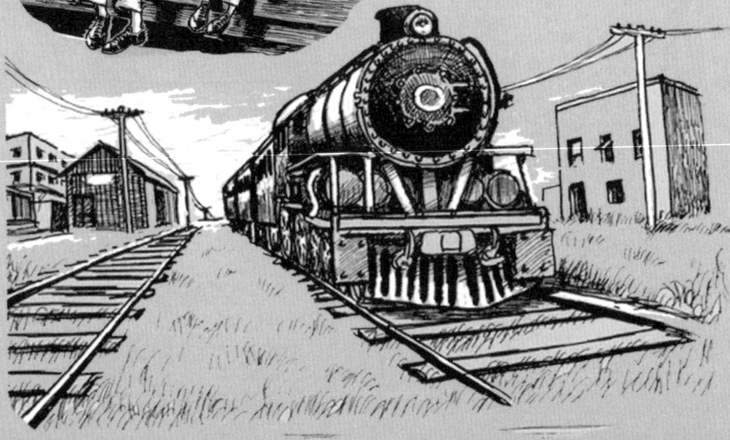